TABLE OF CONTENTS

Custodians Of God's Gift

Bring them up in the discipline and
instruction of the Lord.

Ephesians 6:4

"No matter the label of your style of
parenting, it isn't always going to be smooth,
easy, and graceful.

It is going to be bumpy, challenging, messy, and confusing

The only thing you can always strive to do is to control yourself
no matter what your child chooses to do

Let the power of calm connection lead the way. Truly
relationship building and a "label" to live by."

—Alice Hanscam

WHAT TO EXPECT FROM THIS BOOK

The goal of this book is to focus 100% on you as a parent. After a decade of interacting with teens, pre-teens, my seven and six-year-olds, and mentoring some young adults, I am blessed to have seen the different seasons of each group and the importance of parents in their lives. Hence, I am pleased to share what I have learned with you.

If I were to put it all in four words, I would sum it up as—you are a custodian. Custodians have a lot of work to do because they are entrusted to look out for and take care of something, and that is the entire foundation and framework of this book, regardless of your parental status, a foster parent, single parent, a couple parenting together.

No matter how old your children are, this book will help you become the parent they need. You can't parent someone if you don't know who a parent is and your role. I'm beginning to sound like a broken record, but the intention is to really drill this point that you are called and chosen.

As you read this book, I recommend you follow through with the reflection topics, questions to answer, and stories to reflect on. It will be an interactive experience that will help you understand, implement, and apply the key principles as you parent these gifts from God.

WHAT'S INSIDE

The heart of this book is focused on you as a parent and the key roles you play daily. These roles can be seen in three parts in this book. Each section has four chapters, and each chapter covers a topic in your journey to discover your call as a custodian. The responsibility of becoming a parent shapes your parenting approach. It helps you ask questions about yourself.

How should I interact with my children? What are the best ways to engage them in any situation? What things must I do as a bridge maker? How can I point my children to be responsible adults while under my roof? These are all great questions that will be answered in this book.

Imagine when you just found out you were pregnant with your child, you spend so much time educating yourself on what to expect, what you need to buy, and how you need to prepare: clothing and caregiver options. I want you to spend as much time reviewing the key principles in this book.

In each chapter, you will:

- Know your role as you raise an emotionally intelligent, approachable, spiritual, and friendly child.
- Understand your call to train your children in the way they should go by teaching them to seek God's wisdom and will for their abilities and talents. As they grow up into young adults, your training will be a foundation for your children to build their lives upon.
- Learn the principles that are keys to helping you in your

journey as a parent.

- To empower you to be the adult you want your children to become first.

You are a temporary custodian. You are preparing and equipping yourself to raise your children for a purpose beyond you and your relationship with them. If you notice the use of the word "you" a lot in this book, it's intentional. You are in the front seat, and you are driving.

pa.ren.ting means

1. What we do for our children.
2. Supporting their emotional, social, spiritual, and developmental growth.
3. The process we take to raise our children from babies to the adolescent years.
4. Pointing our children in the direction they should go.

pa.rent means

1. Being a gardener
2. A custodian
3. A mother and a father—biological or guardians

≫ INTRODUCTION ≪

BEFORE THE JOURNEY

The journey of becoming a better parent starts with you.

When we see a diamond, we value the finished product, but behind the scene, a lapidarist is tasked with engraving, cutting, polishing, and cleaning it in its rough state to produce the finished product we see today. Parents are the lapidaries, and our children are the diamonds. We must treasure and value the precious gifts God has given to us: our children, but before we can treasure these gifts, we need to cherish and see the value God sees in us as custodians of these gifts—our children. All parents are custodians. Custodians have a lot of work to do because they are entrusted to look out for and take care of something valuable and nurture everything about that precious jewel.

Imagine having a raw diamond from the ground in your possession and not knowing what to do with it or what tools to use to clean it up. This is what it means to parent a child without knowing the purpose of why you are in your child's life. So, how can you refine this diamond? What tools are needed? Where do you start? The journey of becoming a better parent begins with you.

> Being a parent is a calling and parenting is the work we do towards that calling –
> Toyin Adefemi

Only you can refine your diamonds (children), and the moment you discover and understand your role and the purpose for which you have been called to the office of parenting. It will become meaningful, and you will begin to see the raw diamond as the potential to become something great.

I will refer a lot to you as a custodian, not from a legal sense but from your perspective as a steward, an ambassador, and a representative of God in the lives of your children. You are meant to be a representative of Christ in the lives of your children. I am not saying you must be perfect. Nobody is. You will not know it all. Psalm 32:8 says, " I will instruct you & teach you in the way you should go; I will counsel you with my eye upon you:," this includes parents too.

The journey of this book started when I came to the complete realization that parents—the father and mother—are two individuals who became one. They came together to incubate and birth a child, then the parenting journey began. Parenting is the work we do, the actions we perform, and the emotional rollercoasters we experience while raising these gifts God has given us. However, the focal point of our parenting is to focus on the hearts of our children. To do this, we must first prepare our own hearts.

As a mother of two energetic boys and coach of many parents over the years, I discovered if only we see ourselves as custodians (a temporary parenting status), then our parenting journey, though stressful, would be fulfilling. Our fulfillment comes from knowing we are planting seeds that will harvest when our kids are grown.

What does it take? You must apply grace and understand what your roles are and what they are not. I wish all parents could see themselves from a helicopter view, getting a bigger picture of what parenting is and is not. Take a moment to reflect on your parenting journey so far. Grab a piece of paper and pen and ask yourself the following questions to observe your current state of parenting:

1. What is working for me?
2. What are my struggles as a parent?
3. What is not working?

Then, close your eyes and ask the Creator who placed these gifts (your children) into your life for His help by reflecting on your answers and pray for him to search your heart for areas you can improve on.

Rushing to church one Sunday morning, I was extremely cranky because my boys were dragging their feet and taking their time, knowing we were running late. We arrived at church, and during praise and worship, I felt really bad about hurrying and yelling on my way to God's house. As the preacher began to speak, something dropped into my heart: the purpose of my boys in my life is for them to help me grow in my strengths and work on my weaknesses.

Running late to church was my fault because I woke up late, but the boys' playing wasn't the problem. I just used their playful moment as an excuse to vent, which resulted in me yelling at them. Since I wasn't accountable to myself, my boys held me responsible without speaking a word.

I wonder how often we point fingers at our children instead of taking our actions into consideration. Or if we ever think about what role we could have played, instead of looking at a situation from the lens of our children and not our own. Each child is a gift from God. We are temporary custodians; we don't own them. Our role as custodians is to prepare and train them for a far greater purpose beyond us and our relationship with them.

When we see the bigger picture of our roles, look beyond our children's imperfections, and focus on ourselves, what we say, how we say it, what we do, and how we do it, it can have a lasting impact on our children's lives. Let me put this out there: parenting is not easy because it requires a lot from you. But it isn't going to get easier until you understand the original purpose and why you have been selected to parent this child.

Imagine the parents of Michelle Obama; little did they know they were raising the future first lady of the United States and the first African American woman to rise to that office. My point is we don't know what our children will become, but we must become parents who can guide them to that path; that's what parenting is all about. It's not changing our children's wills. It's not molding them to become someone we could have become. It's not raising them from our viewpoints but from God's view.

Many books on parenting are on the market: how to parent, tips, ideas, seminars, and the list goes on. But there isn't much on parenthood itself. I see a big void in some parenting books. They focus mainly on how you should parent your child, not a lot on the hearts of the parents. Having recognized this, I decided to develop coaching, masterminds, and workshops that focus 100% on helping you purposefully parent your children.

Before you take off with the rest of the chapters, I want to define two important keywords – parenting and parent. Just a disclaimer, this is not a theory or a scientific experiment. These questions are based on my experience, observation in coaching, interactions with other parents, and as a mother.

1. Who is a parent?

2. What is parenting?

3. Who called you?

Starting with the third question – who called you? You have been called to serve as a parent by the Creator Himself—God. He called you to be a custodian of these precious gifts. You don't have to be perfect and know it all, but you need to rely on God as the source in your call to purposefully parent—a calling that is beyond you.

Going back to the two keywords, see this table for the definition:

A PARENT	PARENTING
The calling – You are the custodian of God's gift	The day-to-day activities you do for your child
The title you wear as a Mom and Dad	Focuses on providing for your child's needs, wants, and desires
Emphasizes relationships with everyone in your home	The discipline methods and consequences you apply.
Your parenting style and mindset toward parenting	Giving direction to your child
Focuses on nurturing the child	Teaching them right from wrong

By setting the stage for these two keywords, you can now proceed to the subsequent chapters. Just one request, keep these keywords at the back of your mind as you journey through this book.

LEARN FROM THIS STORY

A couple went to a parenting seminar. During the presentation, they focused so much on each topic from their child's perspective that they totally missed the essence of the workshop to help them parent purposefully.

> An investment in Knowledge
> pays the best interest
> — Benjamin Franklin

As you read this book, see it from your perspective and through your parenting lenses, not those of your children. You can't give what you don't have. You can't give your child love if you don't know what love is. You can't meet your child's needs if you don't know what those needs are.

Lastly, you cannot prepare this child for the future if you don't rely on the One who has called you to do so. Are you ready to embrace God's call upon you to prepare this generation for Him? Are you prepared to develop a deeper principle that will guide you through parenting from God's perspective with His counsel and direction? Let's begin.

Parenting is directing the paths of your child
to find their own paths in life
Toyin Adefemi

»» PART ONE ««

THE CALL

≫ CHAPTER 1 ≪

CHOSEN

You are chosen by God to be your children's parents.
He doesn't make mistake - Unknown

L et's kick off this chapter with Os Guinness's quote, "calling is not only a matter of being and doing what we are but also becoming what we are not yet but are called by God to be." You got married, and the next milestone you and your spouse set is to have children. So you start planning the journey to get pregnant. Or perhaps you were pregnant without even planning it. Whatever the case, the excitement and anticipation of holding your bundle of joy is big.

Next comes the delivery. Your baby is born, and you smile at your bundle of joy, eager to hold him in your arms forever. The excitement of having a baby can be overwhelming. There is immense joy and happiness as you welcome the new member of your family into this world.

It is no longer only about you and your spouse. Now, there's a new person in your life you know nothing about. You don't have information about him, his future, or what lies ahead of you in your parenting journey. The moment you meet your bundle of joy, the calling has begun.

WHAT THE CALL MEANS

> There is a purpose you must fulfil in the life of your child
> — Toyin Adefemi

It is a call to nurture, groom, protect, and train this wonderful soul God has gifted to you and your spouse. This reminds me of when you get married and share your vows with your spouse.

As parents, we don't have a vow but a mandate to raise our children for God's purpose, not ours. Being a parent is far more than having a child or children; your heart is required. "God doesn't call the qualified. He qualifies the called."—Christine Caine.

19

You are qualified for the ministry of parenting. What does it mean to be drawn into the ministry of parenting? The call to parent is about understanding you are preparing your children for God to use as vessels of honor for their generation every day. To become humanitarians, inventors, entrepreneurs, leaders, artists, professionals, and solutions to the needs of their generation.

Start the journey with God in mind. Make Him a part of your parent circle with your spouse. God knows what your children will become in life. He alone knows the future; therefore, only He can guide you in this process.

Now, these are the gifts Christ gave to the church: the apostles, the prophets, the evangelists, and the pastors and teachers. Their responsibility is to equip God's people to do his work and build up the church, the body of Christ. This will continue until we all come to such unity in our faith and knowledge of God's Son that we will be mature in the Lord, measuring up to the full and complete standard of Christ. (Ephesians 4:11-13)

From this Bible verse, see the church as you the parent, and your primary assignment is to prepare and equip your children for God's use and purpose in various roles.

Be a Learner

Fathers and mothers are apprentices who need to apply what they have learned along the way. Dennis Rainey said, "God has a divine purpose in mind when He calls us to be parents." He told a story of their earlier parenting days; he said, "when Denis and his wife, Barbara, were first planning their family, he wrongly assumed God was giving them children to raise. But after years of parenting, he realized the children were to help him finish growing up". Would you agree that our children are teachers and we need to learn from their own viewpoint about life?

> Children learn more from what you are than what you teach
> E.B Dubois

Our children are meant to bring the best out of us and help us with our weaknesses. The moment we realize this, we have unlocked the call to becoming custodians. When I hear parents say, "My child does not listen to me," I pause and think, "Have you been listening to your child?" Let's meditate on Deuteronomy 6:5-9. As you read, replace the word "you" with your name.

> And you must love the Lord your God with all your heart, all your soul, and all your strength. And you must commit yourselves wholeheartedly to these commands that I am giving you today. Repeat them again and again

to your children. Talk about them when you are at home and when you are on the road, when you are going to bed and when you are getting up. Tie them to your hands and wear them on your forehead as reminders. Write them on the doorposts of your house and on your gates.

What does this verse mean, and how does it relate to you as a parent? First, you must love the One who has called you to be a custodian of your child. And then be deeply rooted in His ways. Once you have done that, the next step is repeating what you have learned from God and then transferring it to your children. Remind your child about God's love. Imagine you are consistently walking with God, committing all your ways into His hands, and that He is directing and guiding you in every area of your life, including parenting. Wouldn't that be awesome?

Elizabeth Elizardi, in an article from *Psychology Today*, says,

> Something interesting happens to parents who feel 'called' to raise their children. The higher their sense of calling, the more importance they place on the actual role of parent. And just like those with a calling orientation at work, a higher sense of calling is related to higher personal life satisfaction and work (parenting) satisfaction. The burden of parenting is lower. Such parents experience greater positive affect and lower levels of negative affect.

Parenting does not need to be the best guess. The learning starts with you first, and then your child experiences the benefits of what you have learned.

He Selected You

There are moments when I feel unworthy of being called a mother. One day, I came home from work, and I was extremely agitated about something my boss did that really upset me. Driving home, I was boiling about the situation at work, and I kept replaying it in my mind. Before I knew it, I was pulling into my driveway. I opened the garage door, got out of my car—and there my boys were, very excited to welcome me back home. They were eager to tell me all about what happened to them at school.

I dropped my bag, had zero interest in what they said, and didn't even acknowledge them. I dismissed the excitement by nodding my head and saying: "Mommy had a long day."

My oldest said, "OK, mommy, we get it." His words did not sink in until the next day when I tried to make up by resetting the mood with excitement and a big hug. The little one said, "Mommy, it's OK; we still love you." These words sank to the bottom of my heart.

It is part of God's selection process to choose their father and me as their custodians. Our role is to help them grow, but as we do that, they help us grow. I know I didn't deserve those words, but it didn't make me less of a mother. I learned from that experience.

Why did I share this story? To demonstrate, we don't have to be perfect to be parents. God has selected us with our strengths and weaknesses to raise our children for a special purpose. C.S Lewis said, "You have not chosen one another, but I have chosen you for one another."

What's so amazing is that out of the billion people in the world who could have been your child's parent, God selected you. Isn't it amazing how He chose you to father or mother this precious gift? He finds you trustworthy enough to give you the joy of grooming another human being.

God has not given us a code of parenting or manual to follow; you have to depend on Him. He owns the blueprint of your child's life and will guide you in the process. Your children need to learn from your knowledge and experiences as they grow to become who God has called them to be. There is no such thing as guesswork in this process, but there is something called learning.

Grow in the Process

You do not have to know it all or be perfect to be a part of the selection process. We all have struggles and challenges. "God has chosen you to make you a blessing too many don't blame your situation don't be discouraged don't panic just wait and hold on to God everything has a reason and a season"

(Author Unknown).

When Peter saw Jesus walking on water, he was so excited that he decided to walk on water. But the moment he took his eyes off Jesus, he began to sink. He was distracted by the winds and waves. Like Peter, we will be distracted by behaviors on this parenting journey and may find it challenging to strike the work/life balance. Nevertheless, we should not be discouraged or focus on our weaknesses. It means we are human; we're not perfect. The important thing is to keep going and fix our eyes on Jesus, the Author and Finisher of our lives and faith.

Do It Gracefully

Visualize yourself responding to your children with love when you don't feel like it or have had a very long day. How about responding with love when your child expects you to be upset about something he did wrong? I'm not saying this is easy, but it is worth it. When we apply grace to our parenting, it helps us grow some muscles in patience.

Karis Kimmel Murray pointed out in her book, *Grace Based Parenting Set Your Family Free,*

> Grace is God's unmerited favor. God offers us His favor, not because of what we deserve or because of who we are but who He is. That's how God parents us and why a grace-based home is one where our kids know their identities as loved members of our families don't hinge on their behavior. Again, you don't have to be a perfect

parent; you already aren't. You just have to be a good-enough, grace-based parent.

There are seasons to parenting. Once you master one season, another is around the corner, and the information you learned is outdated. As the seasons change from fall to spring and spring to summer, so will your child change. In a later chapter, I will go into details about each season. You are chosen by the creator to lead, nurture and provide structure for your child. You cannot do it by yourself; you need to lean on the Holy Spirit to guide and direct your decisions, thoughts, and actions. Remember, God chose YOU. His parenting grace - everything you need to raise your child is available to you. Lean on Him.

CHAPTER SUMMARY

- Parenting is a ministry.

- Fathers and mothers are learners, and parenting is applying what you have learned.

- God selected you, and no one else can parent your child any better than you.

- Parenting does not need to be the best guess. The learning starts with you first, and then your child experiences the benefits of what you have learned.

- Do it gracefully.

- It's important to understand you are called for this special assignment, and nobody can do it better than you.

- It is a lot of work emotionally, physically, financially, and psychologically; you must keep one thing in mind: you have been selected by the One who matters.

»CHAPTER 2«

CALLED TO SERVE

Nothing is more important in your life than being one of God's
Tool to form a human soul - Paul David Tripp

Parenthood is all about serving, preparing the hearts of our children, and equipping them for a purpose beyond us and our relationship with them. Let all you do come from a heart of serving.

Your kids may not show how appreciative or thankful they are now, but you will see the fruits of your labor in the future. Keep in mind you are raising a giant for the next generation. Karis Kimmel Murray said: "The theology of parenting is simply this: treat the people you are called to love the way God treats you—with grace." The call to serve includes the grace you have received. That is the same grace you must serve with. It is two-way. God gives us unlimited grace, and, in turn, we must give our children grace too.

You have been hand-picked by God. All you need to raise this child is already hard-wired inside of you. With your strengths and despite your weaknesses, God has given you the assignment to be a custodian of this child. What is the assignment? What is required to fulfill this assignment? How will you be graded? What will be the result? I'm sure other questions are running through your mind; don't worry, we'll get through it in this chapter.

When you think of service, what is the first thing that comes to your mind? Is it activities around the house like cooking, cleaning, laundry, or running errands for the family? Is it being a soccer mom or dad or helping with schoolwork? Don't get me wrong, all these activities are important to keep the family together. I refer to these as servicing the family's needs or providing a service to the family. There is a big difference between servicing and serving. A few weeks ago, I decided to clarify a few questions I had about my parenting ministry. So I decided to go on a 21-day fast to seek God for His guidance.

Two days into the 21-day fast, something dropped in my spirit about servicing and serving. I began to ask what the difference was. To me, they sounded the same. So, I Googled service vs. serving. I intended to find a Bible verse, but I looked for a definition on Google before that. I came across this quote by Simon Sinek "There is a difference between offering a service and being willing to serve. They may both include giving, but only one is generous." This means as parents, you have two functions - being a parent is the serving part, and parenting is the service-providing hat you wear. Serving also means ministering to the needs of our children. By providing spiritual guidance and nurturing their emotional needs. Servicing is the maintenance and how we supply for their physical needs. It is important to understand the difference so you can balance both functions.

PARENTING FROM THE VIEW OF SERVING GOD

You are called to be a servant of God, not a service provider to your children only. Don't let the providing part be more important than you serving God in the lives of your children.

Can you visualize God saying to you, "I need you to represent Me in your home"? How would you feel? Excited? Speechless? Or would you wonder how? Would you feel honored and think, wow, the Creator of the heavens and the earth has called me to serve Him? Then God reminds you of what is in His Word: "And you must commit yourselves wholeheartedly to these commands that I am giving you today. Repeat them again and again to your children. Talk about them when you are at home and when you are on the road, when you are going to bed and when you are getting up" (Deuteronomy 6:6-7).

This is what it means to be a representative of God in our homes. It's about replicating the same relationship we have with Christ in the lives of our children.

> **There is a difference between offering a service and being willing to serve. They may both include giving but only one is generous**
> - *Simon Sinek*

Alright, let me step back. I'm not saying it's going to be easy or smooth. It's a tough call, but as you work out your relationship with God, He will help you overcome the challenges you will experience as a parent. It's going to be daunting and will require a lot from you emotionally, physically, financially, and spiritually. Did I mention the word "growth"? You will grow as your children grow.

Called to Serve as an Ambassador of God

Let's look at the call to serve. It's about becoming a shepherd who leads our children to Christ. And the best news is you don't have to be perfect. You don't have to know it all. You don't need a map. All you need is to be available to be used by God in your child's life.

Ambassadors are members of the president's staff. When they go to foreign countries, they represent the president. Therefore, he does not have to be there physically.

The ambassador serves the president and represents him as well in a country of assignment. Likewise, you are serving your child as an ambassador of Christ. You represent Him daily. Anything outside of this is simply going through the motions without knowing your parenting purpose.

Keep Your Eyes on the One Who Has Called You

This is a key principle every mother and father should follow. The moment you take your eyes off the One who has called you, the weight of parenting becomes heavy.

As parents, sometimes, we will feel exhausted and emotionally drained. Interestingly, these are the very moments our kids will need our attention. They will ask important questions that demand answers and wait for our responses. In our minds, we may think not now and want to dismiss the child. Truly, it might not be the opportune time. But we are custodians, and in our capacity as such, we must learn to control our emotions, see past our own needs, and pay attention to our children. How do we do this? By focusing on God and changing our perspectives.

Ask God for strength, wisdom, and insight under your breath and see the situation from your child's position. Our children will mimic how we behave when we are upset. We must constantly ask God for His help and guidance, especially to produce the fruit of the Spirit: patience when we are triggered to be impatient. Just to give you a sneak preview about trigger, in chapter 7 we will discuss this in length – stay tuned.

Be a Good Example

Your child will mirror you. A couple was arguing, and the wife said something means to her husband in the presence of their child. That same day, this child went to school, and he repeated the very words his mom had said to his dad. The school called both parents to inform them of the word that their child called another child. They were shocked he had repeated the same words used in their morning argument. The point is what you do, your children will repeat.

How should both parents handle this situation, knowing they used the words first and the child simply repeated it in a different context at school? "Let everyone be quick to hear [be a careful, thoughtful listener], slow to speak [a speaker of carefully chosen words and], slow to anger [patient, reflective, forgiving]" (James 1:19).

Be a Teacher and a Learner

> While we try to teach our children all about life, our children teach us what life is all about
> - Angela Schwindt

Angela Schwindt said, "While we try to teach our children all about life, our children teach us what life is all about. It's not just about instilling values, correcting them; it's about growing along the journey with your child." As I'm writing this book, my son is also writing about kids finding their passion and purpose in life. I encouraged him to write since he loves to read books.

Little did I know that his writing would inspire me. One day, he finished his book and was reading it to me. I was like, wow; his story was interesting and easy to follow. So, I went back to my manuscript and revised it to make it more interesting and easier to follow. This is an example of teaching our children something and, in return, learning and gaining another perspective from them.

The call to parenting is a two-way street; we are teachers of our children and also students. We teach them, and we learn from them. Nobody knows it all but what's important is to become a learner.

To Raise Disciples

The number one goal of every father and mother is to raise their child as disciples of Christ. Last year, I read a book by Gary Keller and Jay Papasan called *The One Thing*. As I read the book, I came across this question, "What's the one thing I can do/such that by doing it, everything else will be easier."

I paused and asked myself the same question as a mother. As a mom, my "one thing" was to explain things - especially providing insights, whether spiritual, emotional or others. As parents, we should not assume that our children will understand everything and why they do it. We need to take the time to explain things so it becomes meaningful for them.

> **A Christian parent's number one thing is raising your children as disciples of Christ**
> Toyin Adefemi

Over the years, I have been blessed to interact with hundreds of teenagers and some young adults in faith-based communities, and I ask them about their relationship with God and why they attend Church services. I get different responses. This particular one stands out "my parents make me come to church." The other answer is, "they like hanging around people who share their faith."

At that point, I wasn't a mom, but at the back of my mind, I always knew I didn't want my children to follow me to church without understanding why we go. We apply the "one thing" rule in our home by not assuming our boys know certain things. When we attend church services, we communicate the importance of why we attend church and fellowship with like-minded people. As you raise disciples in your home, take the time to ask them questions about their faith and learn God's word together, this is a key process as you make disciples for Christ.

In 2019, I went on a personal prayer retreat at Sandy Cove in Maryland. I had categories of prayers I wanted to pray about. So I dedicated some time to pray for the kids. I asked the Holy Spirit to help me to be a better mother to my boys. Then the Holy Spirit led me to this Bible verse: "You must love the Lord God with all your heart, all your passion, all your energy, and your every thought. And you must love your neighbor as yourself" (Luke 10:27, The Passion Translation).

As I began to look at this verse, I noticed two important themes: loving God and loving people. When I got back from my trip that night, I immediately taught my boys this verse and had them memorize it. I told them they must love God for themselves, not because of Mommy or Daddy. Of course, boys being boys, they asked fifty million questions.

Imagine children who truly love God and their neighbors. Although we don't know how and when our children will grow to the level of understanding about God, our assignment is to sow the seed of God's Word in their hearts. Let me share with you a key scripture verse that helps me. "I planted the seed in your hearts, and Apollos watered it, but it was God who made it grow" - 1 Corinthians 3:5-6 New Living Translation).

Parenting is a 24/7 assignment from the birth of your child until you die. In every stage and season in your parenting journey, your ultimate goal is to empower your children to be disciples of Christ in and outside of your home.

CHAPTER SUMMARY

- The number one goal of fathers and mothers is to raise their children as disciples of Christ.

- You are called to be a servant of God, not a service provider only. Don't let the providing part be more important than serving God in the lives of your child.

- It's about replicating the same relationship we have with Christ in the lives of our children.

- You are called to serve as ambassadors of God. It's about becoming shepherds who lead our children to Christ.

- Keep your eyes on the One who has called you to serve. This is a key principle for every mother and father to follow.

- Be a teacher and a learner at the same time. Nobody knows it all. What's important is learning as you journey through parenthood.

- Only God can change your child's heart, and that's why you can't go a day without asking Him for His help.

≫ CHAPTER 3 ≪

WHAT IT TAKES

There is no such thing as being the perfect parent.
So just be a real one - Sue Atkins

Have you ever asked yourself what it takes to be a good parent? Has this question crossed your mind at some point in your parenting journey? "A good father is a source of inspiration and self-restraint. A good mother is the root of kindness and humbleness."—Dr. T.P Chia.

Before the arrival of our first son, we had so much freedom. I could go shopping alone, go for walks, and my husband and I can go on dates. This quickly changed when our first son came into the picture. The first wave of reality hit me in the hospital parking lot before we got into the car to take our bundle of joy home. Quick disclaimer, I am used to not opening the car because my hubby opens the door at the time. This was one of my husband's trademarks from our dating years into our marriage - I always felt like a queen in the castle when he does this. This habit soon faded away while at the hospital garage. He had to decide if to open my door or put our newborn into the car. From that day forward, I learned to open and close my own door. No longer could we do what we want without first thinking about how we would prepare for our child. It was a new era of balancing our lives, marriage, and a new baby.

Striking the Balance

> To be a good parent you need to take care of yourself so that you can have the physical and emotional energy to take care of your family
> Michelle Obama

Take care of yourself, so you can take care of your family. It can't be the other way around. If not, you will be burnt out. You're not a robot. Even robots break down, get stuck, and require human intervention from time to time.

In our home, we have this robot cleaner called Cleanbot—thanks to the boys for the beautiful name. We programmed Cleanbot to clean daily, and sometimes we get a notification that Cleanbot is stuck on our phones.

My husband locates and rescues Cleanbot, so it can resume cleaning. My point here is that just like my Cleanbot, you will get stuck somewhere, and you will need to find your way out to continue where you left off. That's part of parenting; we get stuck in some areas of our lives. In fact, life can be overwhelming sometimes due to work, health, death of a loved one, a child with special needs, loss of a job, or marital issues. But our kids still need our attention.

"If you feel burnout setting in, if you feel demoralized and exhausted, it is best for the sake of everyone to withdraw and restore yourself." - Dalai Lama. A couple of years ago, there was a video that went viral on Facebook. A mom was always taking care of everyone in her home except herself. She cooks, cleans, and makes all her children's medical and dental appointments while her husband works to support the home. She started to feel pain, which triggered a visit to the doctors for a health check. Her lab results show she had aggressive cancer spreading in her body, and if she had come six months earlier, they would have removed the cancer cells before it gets to this stage. Don't be too busy that you forget about your own health; it's important to strike a balance.

Sow Daily

God is always on your side. Take a moment to pray first and spiritually fill yourself up with God's Word. If you can't pray at this moment, crack your Bible open or Google Bible verses that will restore your mind. The most powerful assistance every father and mother has is direct access to God, who gave them that child in the first place.

We all have good intentions. We want the best for our children, but it starts with us first. "Sow your seed in the morning and do not be idle with your hands in the evening, for you do not know whether morning or evening planting will succeed, whether this or that, or whether both alike will be good" (Ecclesiastes 11:6, Amplified). A good seed to sow is praying whenever thoughts of your son or daughter cross your mind.

Here are four seeds you can sow daily:
1. S – scriptures
2. E – encouragement
3. E – empathy
4. D – dedicating time daily to your son or daughter

These four seeds should not be subject to your child's behavior or attitude toward you in the morning. Sow them always. It's all about you extending the gift of grace God gives you daily to your children. God's love for us is unconditional, so our love for our children should be unconditional as well.

Your Words Are Powerful

A frustrated mom once said to Jackie, a family friend, she's tired and giving up on her teenage son because he is not listening, has bad grades, is selfish, and the list goes on. She concluded the conversation by saying that "he will not be anything in life; he will turn out like his father, and she's only wasting her time—her son has pushed her buttons to the edge." Words have power. "Remember that the most important thing is not your child's behavior. The most important thing is your child. Look beyond behavior and connect with your child."—Issa Waters. There are many ways to be firm and get your message across without breaking your children's spirit.

Jackie's heart melted because the boy was so hurt by those words—his facial expression said it all. Jackie made several attempts to connect to the mom and help her see differently through the eyes of grace. But she had already made up her mind she was giving up on the boy. Jackie tried and tried to convince the mother, but to no avail.

Looking at this story, I empathize with the mom and the teenage son. The parent/child relationship has its challenges, but giving up is not an option. "Behind every young child who believes in himself is a parent who believed first." - Mathew Jacobsen.

> **No matter how young or old we are, the voices around us produce a lasting impact.**
> Jed Jurchenko

You can't abandon the ship because it is wrecked. You have to attempt to put the pieces together or find someone who can help.

Time and Patience

The psalmist says, "Help us to remember that our days are numbered and help us to interpret our lives correctly. Set your wisdom deeply in our hearts" (Psalm 90:12), The Passion Translation). One of the requirements for Moms and Dads is time. Why time? It takes time to interact with your children. It takes time for you to listen to them, to help them with something. Let me use a word we are familiar with: currency. It's an exchange for an item, product, system, or service.

The currency all parents can give their children is time—a valuable investment in your child's life. I am using money in the context of value and what you are familiar with. The currency of parenting is not the money or the things we buy for them, but what's most important is our daily interactions with them.

A mom once said when her son asks her for help with his homework, it takes a lot out of her. She would prefer to give him the answers than spend another hour and a half with him. Another mom said it is easier to do the chores than assigning them to her teenage daughter because it requires a lot to even get her to do them in the first place. Abigail Van Buren says, "If you want your children to turn out well, spend twice as much time with them and half as much money."

As a custodian, you cannot connect by buying things to express your care; building a relationship is more valuable. I follow a lady on youtube; she is a reputable and successful entrepreneur and a leader of an organization. She is a bank CEO, a pastor, an author, an entrepreneur, and has a business she started in her twenties. One of the core values she holds on to is communicating with her family. Regardless of where she is in the world or what she is doing, she takes time to connect with her children. When her kids became toddlers, she spent less time traveling worldwide to be closer to home. One day, her daughter said, "Mommy, I know you're very busy. I know you have a lot on your plate, but one thing I want you to do for me is I want you to shower me every night."

So the mom made a promise to shower her every night. Her daughter looked forward to this daily because it was their special moment to bond. The mom has found a currency that is very valuable to her daughter. It is quality time.

As parents, entrepreneurs, career-oriented, or business owners, you will never be less busy. You are not going to have more time than 24 hours. Therefore, you must work on managing your time wisely to accommodate the gifts God has given you. Perhaps you're thinking, how is that possible? Where is the time? There is always time; you have to look at your busy schedule. You have to arrange and move things around to spend special time with your children daily. For some parents, it's at dinner time while for others, it is studying together or reading a book a few times a week together. Investing in your children's lives is one of the important things of being a parent. As you spend quality time together, you learn more about each other.

> **Each day in our lives we make deposits
> in the memory banks of our children**
> — *Charles R Swindoll*

The story of the busy mom I shared with you earlier is a great example of striking a balance. She found her balance, and she has learned to manage her workload and busy life. Hence, she creates room for her kids on a nightly basis. Your children may not remember every word you speak to them or how you said it, but they will remember how you connected with them.

They will never forget the time you took to be with them to ensure they got your message loud and clear. It's not the length of time you spend with your son or daughter that counts but the quality of time you invest in listening that makes the difference.

CHAPTER SUMMARY

- You don't have as much freedom as you did when you did before the arrival of your children. You now have another human being to account for. It's a new era of balancing your life, marriage, and child.

- It's about taking care of yourself, so you can take care of your family. Take care of yourself, including your emotions, spiritual life, physical and mental health.

- You are not alone; God is always on your side. As I said earlier, the most powerful assistance every father and mother has is access to God, who gave you that child in the first place.

- It is a big responsibility, and it takes your heart to do it well.

- Parenting requires faith and works. When you sow a seed, you don't see the results right away. It takes time for that seed to mix up with the soil, break through the soil, and spring up. That is the faith part of parenting.

»CHAPTER 4«

BE PURPOSEFUL

The highest privilege and purpose as a parent is to lead the child in the way of Christ - Max Lucado

Parenting is about laying the right foundation in every season and every stage of a child's life. It makes it more purposeful for you. Every involvement, every action, every prayer, every seed of love poured into the life of your child will go far and deeply root them into a solid foundation as they grow. This is why God made you the custodian of your children.

The Blueprint

Let's review the idea of a blueprint. God has the blueprint for all children, which includes a plan of who they are now and who they will become in the future. You don't have the full blueprint, but you know the One who holds it. As you seek God, you learn more and more about the parenting blueprints. Not every child is the same, so you need to learn the uniqueness in each child.

You are a temporary custodian. The key tools your children need are good blueprints for them to build upon when they grow up. God placed you as a custodian to put your children on the path to finding and fulfilling their purposes. It is important to ask this question—what examples can our children learn from our lives that will become blueprints they can follow? Once you understand this basic foundation, the next question is, how is this possible? It all begins with laying a strong foundation.

Laying the Foundation

In the Bible, there is a story of a man called Job. He was wealthy in every area, but laying the right foundation in his home was important. Let's see how. Here is an assessment of Job's net worth:

> "He owned 7,000 sheep, 3,000 camels, 500 teams of oxen, and 500 female donkeys. He also had many servants. He was, in fact, the richest person in that entire area" (Job 1:3).

I am sure his kids were admired by other kids in their neighborhood and community. They were known as the coolest and richest kids in the block. Picture yourself as one of Job's neighbors.

> "Job's sons would take turns preparing feasts in their homes, and they would also invite their three sisters to celebrate with them" (Job 1:4).

Job had it all. His kids got along well, and there was much love and unity in the family. A purposeful home has unity and love, even though there will be moments when you all disagree, but the harmony is stronger than the disagreements. Continuing with the case study of Job, he laid a key foundation for them see Jobs 1 verse 5 for that foundation.

> "When these celebrations ended—sometimes after several days—Job would purify his children. He would get up early in the morning and offer a burnt offering for each of them. For Job said to himself, "Perhaps my children have sinned and have cursed God in their hearts." This was Job's regular practice. (Job 1:5).

Job understood it wasn't about the money or fame he and his children had. It was not about their last name or his influence in the community to help his children secure a better future. Job understood his purpose as a parent and a custodian of God's gifts. He knew that involved always praying for them. Job chose their birthdays to offer thanksgiving on their behalf to God.

Before your children grow up, before they fully understand their faith, you must stand in the gap for them until they have a deep relationship with Christ. Job knew the greatest asset wasn't his money but laying a strong foundation of praying on their behalf to God.

Apply Wisdom

"The mind of the prudent [always] acquires knowledge, And the ear of the wise [always] seeks knowledge" (Proverbs 18:15). Parenting is tough, and it's tough because you are nurturing another human being. Your child may be a reflection of you in some areas or in all areas. What you do and how you do it will shape their understanding of life from your viewpoint. That's why it is important to apply wisdom. What is wisdom? It is having good judgment and making decisions that will help you and your child to grow. How do you get wisdom? Ask God who gives it freely (James 1:5). How can you apply wisdom-based parenting? Katie Gerten answers this question:

> Respond to your children with love in their worst moments, their broken moments, their selfish moments, their lonely moments, their frustrating moments, their inconvenient moments because it is in their most unlovable human moments that they most need to feel loved.

It's all about wisdom, not responding with emotions. You can't do it alone. You need God to help you daily. A great example is the Prodigal Son's father. The prodigal son asked his father for his portion of the father's inheritance. After receiving the estate, the prodigal son went away and splurged it all. He mismanaged his assets and the money his father worked hard for. One day, the son came back to his senses, and he decided to return home.

On the boy's way home, his father sees his son coming after making the biggest mistake of his life and looking like a poor boy. The father met the son halfway and threw him a party to welcome him home. He chose to apply wisdom to an uncomfortable situation. His son knew he didn't deserve it; yet,

> **Not speaking about everything is a great way of applying wisdom. Unspoken words echo a stronger message to your child in their lowest moments.**
>
> Toyin Adefemi

his father decided to show him, love.

It Takes Time

Before you can plant a seed, it must be inside you as a parent. Annette Breedlove talks about seeding from the child and parent's perspective. She says,

> The very reason to plant seed is to produce a harvest. We don't sow seed just to let it grow without picking the wonderful fruit or vegetables that come from it. The

harvest, or crop, out of our life is God's work in us and through us designed to impact others. Sometimes, the hardest thing as a parent is to know if the seeds we have sown are taking root in the heart of our children. Be encouraged that although the fruit isn't always seen right away in our kids, there is a period of growth while the roots are digging deep.

Parenting is planting good seeds daily into the hearts of our children. Sowing good seeds involve connecting with our children positively, showing them love, and spending time with them. Disciplining them in love is also a part of it. You may think it's impossible, but it's not. To succeed, we must rely on the One who has called us to be the custodians of the gifts He has placed in our hands.

Every generation will say parenting is very hard. But sometimes, what needs to change is our source of help. We need to rely on God rather than ourselves. Let me say this: your words are seeds that have the power to make or break your child's spirit. What you speak to your teenagers will grow in their hearts. So you had better be conscious of your need for godly wisdom to navigate these times.

If you want to be an influencer in your children's lives, invest your time in them. If you invest time in the life of your child, you will reap the reward. Also, the more time you spend with them, the more you will all learn about each other.

Types of seeds to sow:

1. Morals
2. Integrity
3. Being emotionally intelligent
4. Being a responsible citizen
5. Self-Confidence
6. Love of God
7. Honesty and kindness
8. Telling the truth

There was an interview with an important man. He said when he was young, his father would give him a newspaper to read. He didn't understand why his father would call him to read newspapers with him every evening at the same time. During this time spent with his father at a young age, he cultivated reading habits. Little did his father know that this seed he was planting in his son's life would one day bring him before nations and presidents.

Giving a gift can open doors; it provides access to important people. All you need is to be intentional, conscious, purposeful, and mindful.

REFLECTION

1. Take some time to pray and reflect on what blueprints you need, ways you can lay a strong foundation in your

home - like Job did and how you can apply wisdom in all your interaction with each child.

2. What can you do more of and less of?

_____
_____
_____
_____
_____
_____
_____
_____
_____

That's what purposefully parenting is all about. It's about being consistent regardless of what may come your way or in your moments of imperfection. God didn't call you to parent because you are perfect. He called you to parent your children for Him. If only we can take our eyes away from ourselves and our children and see the Holy Spirit as our mentor, counselor, and navigator, then parenting wouldn't be so stressful.

CHAPTER SUMMARY

- Parenting is about laying the right foundation in every season, every stage of the child's life.
- God has the blueprint for all children, including designing a plan of what they are now and what they will become in the future.
- The first layer of foundation is God's Word
- Apply wisdom to your parenting. You can't do it alone; you need God to help you daily.
- Parenting is sowing seeds without seeing the results now but later when your children grow up.
- What needs to change is our dependency on God and not ourselves. Your words have the power to make or break your child's spirit.
- To be an influencer in your child's life, you must invest your time. If you invest time in the life of your child, you will reap the reward.

"Whatever you do [no matter what it is] in word or deed, do everything in the name of the Lord Jesus [and in dependence on Him], giving thanks to God the Father through Him" (Colossians 3:17).

≫ PART TWO ≪

THE PILLARS NEEDED

»CHAPTER 5«

BUILDING THE RIGHT PILLARS

The goal of parenting isn't to create perfect kids.
It's to point our kids to the perfect God - Lindsey Bell

Parenting is directing our children to find their own paths in life. As a mom and dad, you have two roles to play in your children's lives. The first one is nurturing them and providing structure at the same time. You cannot apply one and not the other. It requires a balanced approach with your child.

In a movie production team, you have a director, a producer, and the actors. The role of the director is to guide the actors and ensure they capture the true essence of the play. They are in charge of the expressions, the emotions, and the artistic aspects of that play to make sure it's real and comes to life. The director works behind the scenes and is responsible for the success of the movie. The producer is in charge of the operations, hiring, coordination, scheduling the finances, raising funds, and anything that has to do with the operation of the movie.

> **Parenting is directing our children to find their own paths in life**
> - Toyin Adefemi

The actors are responsible for acting out the roles they are assigned. If the director and producer are not on the same page, they will not produce their best. In the context of parenting, the director is the Holy Spirit who oversees the entire success of your children's lives while you are the producer who is charged with the day-to-day operations of the movie; the actors are your children. Whatever script you give them, they will play by.

It takes a lot to raise children, and sometimes, as my husband and I raise our own, we ask ourselves if we are really making an impact, a difference in the lives of our handsome boys. So we came up with pillars to assess our parenting journey. Here are the six parenting pillars:

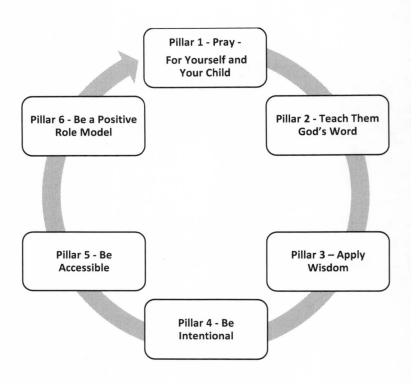

Pillar 1 - Pray for yourself and your child

In the previous chapter, I spoke about Job when he had it all: money, wealth, riches, fame, and everything. But Job understood his children needed God more than what he could give, so he would offer sacrifices on behalf of his children for mercy and forgiveness from God. How are you dedicating your child to God daily? My goal is not to guilt-trip you but to make you aware the biggest part of becoming a parent is to be a servant leader.

Pray for God's will to prevail in their lives daily, for them to long for and love the Lord, and for them to love the Lord with all their hearts, minds, and souls. Imagine every parent seeking God's face on behalf of their children. We will cultivate love, grace, and everything missing in our society today into their hearts by God's grace. "Call to me and I will answer you, and will tell you great and hidden things that you have not known" (Jeremiah 33:3).

A friend and I talked the other day about men of God who have done great things in this world. For example, Billy Graham, his parents did not know there were raising an evangelist who would win millions of souls for God. The parents of Moses in the Bible did not know they were raising the deliverer for the nation of Israel. Rachel in the Bible did not know she was raising Jacob, who would eventually give birth to the children of Israel, and God would fulfill His promises to Abram through Jacob's generation.

You don't know what the future looks like for your kids; that's why it is important to be intentional in praying daily for them and their future. It is planting a seed in the place of prayer, which will one day become a tree providing shade for the people around it. Don't get distracted.

We cannot raise our children for God's purpose on our own. We need the Holy Spirit's help to be better Moms and Dads. His strength will be perfect in our weak areas. It is not about imposing your will but God's will. God has entrusted these children into our hands, not for us to fulfill our wills and goals or what we think is best for them but to accomplish God's desire for each child.

Pillar 2 - Teach them God's Word

Our children should not wait every Sunday or during small groups to learn the Word of God. God's Word should be read and meditated upon in our homes. We should fellowship together as a family. The most valuable gifts we can give to our children are not the toys, shoes, clothes, money, or phones but God's Word and prayer that will sustain them in their lifetime. We must become like Philip in the story of the Ethiopian eunuch in Acts 8:26–31:

> Then the Lord's angel said to Philip, "Now go south from Jerusalem on the desert road to Gaza." He left immediately on his assignment. Along the way, he encountered an Ethiopian who believed in the God of the Jews, who was the minister of finance for Candace, queen of Ethiopia. He was on his way home from worshiping God in Jerusalem. As he rode along in his chariot, he was reading from the scroll of Isaiah.
>
> The Holy Spirit said to Philip, "Go and walk alongside the

chariot." So Philip ran to catch up. As he drew closer, he overheard the man reading from the scroll of Isaiah the prophet. Philip asked him, "Sir, do you understand what you're reading?" The man answered, "How can I possibly make sense of this without someone explaining it to me?" So he invited Philip up into his chariot to sit with him. (The Passion Translation)

Let me break down some of the parenting insights from this story. Philip was available and led by the Spirit of God. Being led by the Holy Spirit is an important principle to live by when raising children. We do not know what they are thinking or doing at all times, but the One who created them knows everything about them. Therefore, it is necessary to be led by the Holy Spirit, allowing Him to be a part of our parenting experience. This story points out something valuable, Phillip helped the Ethiopian guy to understand what he was reading. Your children have questions, and they need someone who has been there to help them. These are moments that are so precious, and they will shape your child's understanding of God's word.

Pillar 3 – Use Wisdom

We must give the Holy Spirit full access to how we parent. In return, He will give us wisdom. If Phillip was not available, would the Ethiopian eunuch understand God's Word? The key question from this story is, "How can I possibly make sense of this without someone explaining it to me?" We must teach our children God's Word. This is a significant role we play as custodians. The critical ingredient you need is wisdom.

> The Spirit of Yahweh will rest upon him, the Spirit of Extraordinary Wisdom, the Spirit of Perfect Understanding, the Spirit of Wise Strategy, the Spirit of Mighty Power, the Spirit of Revelation, and the Spirit of the Fear of Yahweh. (Isaiah 11:2, The Passion Translation)

Do you need the wisdom to guide you through better parenting? Take a moment to talk to God and ask Him for help.

Pillar 4 - Be Intentional

As a millennial parent myself, I understand we are distracted by technology, social media, and busy with work and our goals and all of this. But it is important not to allow our business to sidetrack us from cultivating positive seeds into our children's lives. As I said before, there is no parenting manual. No compass or map comes with each child. Imagine if God had a manual on how to raise children.

What would it be like? I envision a world of clones; each child would be the same. And that's not what God intended. Every child is unique and has something God is pleased with to fulfill in this world.

Pillar 5 – Be Accessible

Make yourself available at all times. Don't be too busy that you don't know what is going on in their world. Don't brush them off when they want to speak to you. The matter may seem trivial to you, but the mere fact that they are bringing it up is a sign it is important to them. Create an environment and demeanor that makes your child comfortable enough to speak to you about anything. Their well-being must be your top priority.

During your day, check on your teenager. Send her a scripture, words of affirmation, and do a random check-in during your day. Pay close attention to what is going on in her world. For example, sports, dance, events, or recitals. Never violate these two rules:

1. Don't miss any of their important events at school or otherwise.
2. Don't start a conversation when you have limited time.

Pillar 6 – Be a Positive Role Model

When you ask a teenager, who is your role model? you hardly hear, "my parents." Parents, you are the first role models your teens will have in their adolescent years. They will watch you, hold on to your words, and learn your ways. After all, you are the person they see most. If you lie, cheat, gossip, or are negative, you will rub off some of this behavior on them. I was talking to a parent who had concerns about her teenage son one day.

For thirty minutes, she went on and on about everything he was doing wrong—his this, his that. Having been in teens ministry for so long, I quickly realized that the mother was the problem, not the son. She was so focused on the negatives she could not appreciate the positive things he did. Don't just talk the talk; show it by being a good and positive example.

She pointed many fingers at her son. But the truth is the anger she felt because of her failed marriage had clouded her perspective. She wanted him to listen to her, but she didn't listen to me when I tried to get her to look at his point of view. She was asking him for something she was not willing to do – which is to listen. Listening is a two-way street. It doesn't mean you will lose your parental authority.

It is critical to raise up your children with good values. You must walk the walk and lead by example at the same time. In return, you will earn your children's respect and admiration and be their role model.

REFLECTION

Using the circle in question one, identify what your strong pillars are. Which pillar do you need to work on improving?

1.   Identify your most challenging pillar. Think about why it is so difficult? In what ways can you improve these pillars?

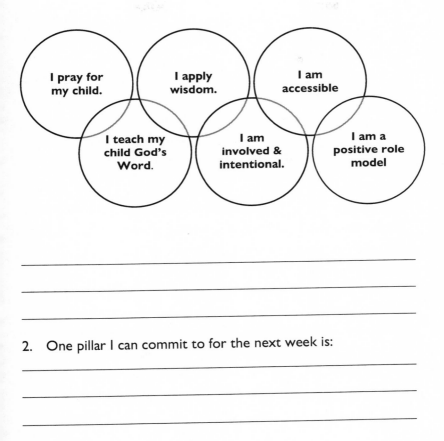

I pray for my child.

I apply wisdom.

I am accessible

I teach my child God's Word.

I am involved & intentional.

I am a positive role model

_____

_____

_____

2. One pillar I can commit to for the next week is:

_____

_____

_____

CHAPTER SUMMARY

- Pray for Your Child – For God's will to prevail in their lives daily, for them to long for and love the Lord, for all the children to love the Lord with all their hearts, all their minds, and all of their souls.

- Teach them God's Word –The most valuable gifts we can give to our children are not the toys, shoes, clothes, money, and phones but God's Word and prayer that will sustain them in their lifetime.

- Apply Wisdom – The critical ingredient you need is wisdom.

- Be Intentional – Every child is unique and has something God is pleased with inside to fulfill in this world.

- Be Accessible – Part of your priorities is to put their well-being at the top of your list of priorities.

- Be a Positive Role Model – It is critical to raise your children with good values. You must walk the walk and lead by example at the same time. In return, you will earn your children's respect and admiration and be their role model.

≫CHAPTER 6≪

YOU ARE A MIRROR

Children are like a mirror. They help you see yourself and all the
flaws that you and your partner might have avoided
looking at earlier - Virginia Clinton Kelley

You can buy clothes for your children. You can provide food for them. You can meet their needs and desires. But you cannot protect their destinies. You don't know who they will become. The important thing is to know the One who holds the keys to their future. Your Walk with God Is Important. One thing you must do is personally get closer to God. I remember a story of someone whose son started kindergarten. He was always sheltered in a faith-based setting, even daycare.

They always protected him, and he was very passionate about the things of God, as little as he was. On his first day of kindergarten, when he came back home, his mom noticed some changes in his words. He described one of his classmates as a fat person. His mother was very shocked and tried to correct him. She told him not to call anyone fat or other names.

He said to his mom, "But she is fat."

His mom started crying that her little boy was now in the real world. He went on to say some not-so-nice words. While clearing his book bag, the same week, his mom came across a picture of a boy dressed as a girl. His teacher asked him to draw a picture of someone. He drew a picture of a boy in a skirt because it was funny, and he wanted to laugh with his friends.

His mom was heartbroken. Still, in shock that her son was changing in the first week of school, she cried and got on her knees to pray for him. She prayed he would be a light to his classmates and not be changed by the people around him. After prayer, she received notification on her Gmail of a devotional and a prayer book. The title was *Praying for Your Kindergartener on Their First Week of School*. She busted out crying and was so overwhelmed with joy that God answered every prayer, no matter how short it was. Is'nt so refreshing how God can use an email to take away a concerned parent's pain?

She read the devotional, and it had clues on ways to pray for her son in his first week of school. From that moment on, the mom asked God to help her to be sensitive spiritually.

You may be wondering why I shared this and what I want

to point out from this story. The main point is we must maintain a close relationship with God. When our children step foot into the educational system, they will be surrounded by all kinds of influences, sometimes good or bad. As I said before, you cannot be with your children every second of the day, but the Holy Spirit can. Hence, prayer is absolutely vital. You don't know the future, but you know God, who knows tomorrow and beyond.

Your State of Mind

Juan Sanchez said,

> We cannot pass on to our children what is not first in our own hearts (Deut. 6:6). This means that moms, dads, grandparents, teachers, ALL of us must saturate ourselves in the Word of God. We must seek God and thirst after God as in a dry and weary land (Psalm 63:1). And where has God revealed Himself but in His Word? We must continually listen to and receive God's instruction in His Word as illuminated by the Holy Spirit of God.

It breaks my heart when parents don't pray for their children. It is a key ingredient to parenting God's way. Going back to the story of the mom and her Kindergartener son, she would have been so frustrated and cranky around the house towards her son. In her emotional state of mind, she drew closer to God, her state of mind shifted towards prayer. A solution-based approach to everything.

You are a Mirror

Our children are like sponges; they soak what they see in you. Do not forget this. Everything you do is viewed and internalized by your child. Are you a grateful person? Are you happy with your life? The love you have for yourself will reflect in the life of your child. So you must spend time working on yourself as you evolve, discover, and maximize your potential.

One of the unique things about my husband and me is we believe in serving in the church. My husband serves in the music ministry, and I serve in the teens' ministry. Our boys see us doing this every Sunday, so they said when they grow up, they want to serve God too. This is a good example of serving and letting your children see and aspire to mirror you. I use a mirror as an example, not for you to pretend to be perfect or put up a front but to make you aware your children are watching you.

Invest in Your Health

An empty person cannot give anything valuable to her children. Self-care is very important, especially in the area of mental health. For example, if you are cranky, everyone in your house will get a dose of it. During this time, you will say things you don't mean. Our children will internalize these words.

If possible, ask for help. Ask your close friends and family. Take some time during the week or daily, depending on your schedule to examine your life. It is important to guard your heart and do so with all diligence (Proverbs 4:23). My alone time - my quiet time with God is right before the entire house gets up. I get up and cry if I need to, or I stay in the presence of God for Him to fill me up.

Learn to separate your role as a wife, corporate worker, and entrepreneur from your role as a mother or father. How can you balance work, life, and parenting at the same time? You must learn to separate each aspect of your roles and responsibilities and then prioritize each one.

I was speaking to my seven-year-old recently about an argument, and he said, "Mommy, I haven't seen you and Daddy argue before." I smiled because I know my husband and I argue just as other couples do. But we do not do it in the presence of our children. We have learned to separate our marriage, parenting, and work-life from each other to keep a drama-free home as much as possible. In chapter 3, I shared a story of a mom. Here is a recap – the mom takes care of everyone's appointments while her husband works to support the home. She started to feel pain, which triggered a visit to the doctors for a health check. Her lab results came back with stage four cancer. Then the doctor looked up and said, "madam, if you had come six months earlier, we would have removed the cancer cells." Invest in your health so you can reap the fruits of your labor in the future.

Don't Repeat the negative principles in your upbringing.

I was not given the best attention while growing up. My parents divorced when I was six years old, and I was partially raised by my grandma, who I visited a couple of times in a year. During this period in my young days, I was lonely. I felt unloved, uncared for, and was molested. To top it all off, I was this shy girl who had reading challenges too. In my teen years, I was very insecure and had zero self-confidence.

I had many lonely days and contemplated suicide twice in my teenage years. In a counseling session with tears flowing down my face, I remember saying that I hated life, everything in it, and some family members. I felt I was robbed of my childhood because of my parents' divorce. It took the power of the Holy Spirit to completely help me let go of the past. I knew with His help, I could rewrite my own story by becoming that mom who understands her role as a custodian of God's gifts. This is one of the reasons I decided to write this book. It is for you to see your role beyond you and see it as a calling for you to be a temporary custodian of your child.

As you proceed in your journey as a mom or a dad, avoid visiting the past and carrying those traits you saw in your parents, which you hated. In the next chapter, you will learn about triggers - external and internal. The situation in our childhood can trigger some internal feelings from our childhood, so it is important to watch out and get help if they are negative and are becoming a barrier to your parenting,

PARENTING STYLES AND HOW THEY AFFECT YOUR CHILD

Can you picture a child who is independent, self-reliant, socially accepted, academically successful, empathetic, well-behaved, and skilled at discussions and negotiations? A child who is a proficient problem solver, always satisfied with whatever they are being given, approachable, and cooperative with their parents. Sounds like a perfect child, right? But really, there is no such thing. Your child will pick up some of these traits from you, but it depends on your parenting style.

Every Christian parent's heart, mind, and soul echoes 3 John 1:14. You can agree that you want your children to walk in the truth. It is your prayer, hope, and desire. The deal is that your parenting style plays a significant role in your children's lives and how they walk in the truth. Have you heard of the *5 Love Languages* by Gary Chapman, personality assessments – choleric, sanguine, melancholic, and others? Then you are in the right lane.

If I tell you that parenting and teaching are related, would you believe me? Think about this quote for a second: "Parents are teachers, and home is a child's first and most important classroom."—Hillary Clinton. The way you interact with your children and your relationship with them is critical to their growth. It is important to ensure your parenting style is supporting the healthy growth and development of your child.

Types of Parenting Styles

1. Permissive Style
   - Provides few rules and rarely disciplines
   - Friendship instead of parenting
   - Has minimal expectations, and children are given few directions
2. Authoritarian Style
   - Communication is mostly one-way
   - Little room for negotiation, rarely allow their children to make their own choices
   - Affection and praise are seldom given
3. Uninvolved/Neglectful Style
   - Overwhelmed by life problems, ignores their children
   - Communication is limited
   - Shows minimal warmth, love, and affection to their children
4. Authoritative Style
   - Sets limits and enforces rules
   - Listens to their child's requests and questions
   - Has discussions and negotiations

5. Your child's outcome will largely depend on your parenting style, either as an authoritative parent where discipline, communication, and nurturing are critical, a permissive parent, where you are mostly indulgent, and the rules are overly relaxed or non-existent, an authoritarian where discipline is most important, and the children cannot

understand the rules; they only follow them blindly. Or you will be an uninvolved parent who is not interested in parenting or is unsure of what to do. Hence, you do nothing and set no boundaries or principles to follow.

CHAPTER SUMMARY

- Your walk with God is important. Parents must have a closer walk with God. You don't know the future, but you know God, who knows tomorrow and beyond.

- You are a mirror. Our children are like sponges. They soak what they see in us. Do not forget this. Everything you do is viewed and internalized by your child.

- Invest in your health. An empty person cannot give anything valuable to her child. Self-care is very important, especially in the area of mental health.

- Don't repeat the negative principle in your upbringing. As you proceed in your journey, it is important to avoid visiting the past and carrying those traits you saw in your parents, which you hated.

- Parenting Styles and How They Affect Your Child

- Parenting and teaching are related. You may not have a physical classroom, but your home is one.

- Four Types of Parenting Styles
    - Permissive
    - Authoritarian
    - Uninvolved
    - Authoritative

»CHAPTER 7«

TRIGGERED

Between stimulus and response, there is a space.
In that space lies our freedom and power to choose our response.
In our response lies our growth and freedom
- Viktor E. Frankl

When triggered, your emotions tell you something about you, not about your children or what they did. Parenting is about you managing your feelings, having an awareness of your feelings, thoughts, and how you respond, not react. As custodians, managing and controlling your emotions when interacting with your child is key to purposefully parenting.

The previous chapter talked about the four parenting styles: authoritative, authoritarian, permissive, and uninvolved. It is important to ensure your parenting style is supporting the healthy growth and development of your children. The way you interact with your children and your relationship is very important to their growth. Regardless of your parenting style, you will be triggered by your children.

What does it mean to be triggered? What words come to mind when you think of parenting triggers? Parenting triggers can be described as super reactive spots from within you that are activated by your child's words, behaviors, attitudes, or comments. A trigger may also be anything you experience in the present that starts a feeling from the past (Laura Markham, Clinical Psychologist).

UNDERSTANDING YOUR PARENTING TRIGGERS

> **Behavior is how young children communicate. It's up to us to interpret their feelings and needs**
> — Allison Reese

Most times, as parents, we let our emotions get the best of us. Our children often push those buttons we didn't even know we had, and before we know it, we start yelling at the top of our lungs. We get irritated or upset, lash out and go from 0 – 10 on the rage scale in a matter of seconds. Before you know it, you cannot control your emotions.

The truth is that sometimes as parents, our children remind us of ourselves and the very things we don't like about us. Therefore, when we see them exhibiting those behaviors, it becomes a trigger, and we flare up at the slightest display. Other triggers may be childhood experiences, a long day at work, or a seeming lack of connection between you and your child.

Taking a deeper dive

Parenting puts a spotlight on you, and the audience is your family. They get to see you outside of the public view, and they see it all: your weak or strong moments. Hence, it is crucial to be aware of your triggers. Do you find yourself always yelling or responding in anger or frustration? Are you tired of yelling at your kids—young or old? You do not need to dig too much into your past to determine what's really bothering you. It could be the little things such as not getting a thank you after doing something for your kids or they are not listening when you speak to them.

These are universal behaviors and not necessarily deep-rooted problems you need to stress; no one likes to go unnoticed. And nobody likes being unappreciated after helping someone. Therefore, to encourage you to be aware of these triggers, instead of focusing on your child's behavior, let's keep the spotlight on you; as you identify your triggers.

REFLECTION QUESTIONS

Reflect on a situation when you felt worked up recently by something your child did. What did they say or do that triggered you to get upset, hurt, or angry?

1. What was it?

    _____

    _____

    _____

    _____

    _____

2. How did you feel?

    _____

    _____

    _____

    _____

    _____

    _____

    _____

3. Which of the descriptions listed in figure 2.1 triggers you the most?

    _____

    _____

    _____

    _____

    _____

Doesn't eat enough or eats too much	Makes loud noises	Whining or nagging
Siblings fighting	Crying nonstop	Argues talks back
Messy room	Yelling	Throws tantrums
Interrupts your conversations	Meltdowns or embarrasses you	Not organized
Bad attitude	Self entitlements	Ungrateful or disrespectful

Figure 2.1

Be Self-aware

What do you do when your child says something, and it throws you off? Or what do you do when you are upset and lose it? When you respond to your children, do so appropriately. You have more self-control than them. You are an adult, and they are children; therefore, it is important to positively influence their behaviors by checking your emotions.

Because your child has a wrong attitude, meltdowns, or throws tantrums does not mean you should join them. It is best to respond by being calm, not raising your voice, and being reasonable about whatever the issue might be. I remember using this tool at a workshop.

One of the parents mentioned that the word "mom" triggers her because her children call her nonstop. The audience laughed, but I can relate, especially when you have multiple kids with small age gaps in between them. Another parent asked what if your children know your triggers and purposely use them against you. My advice to this parent was to make sure what your children think is a trigger is no longer important. So when the kids are trying to use her trigger against her, she can go with the flow and let them know it no longer affects her.

Seven Essential Factors for Trigger-Free Parenting

1. Become aware of the triggers. Write down your feelings to understand yourself better and why certain behaviors get you upset.
2. Be a calm parent. Create a parent proof that you will not lash out or explode regardless of the behavior.
3. Strive toward responding calmly.
4. Pray and ask for help. Pause, step back and think about a softer response by asking for grace.
5. Try and say words that will build up your children without tearing down their self-esteem. As parents, being careful about the words we say to our children is

of the utmost importance. Constant insults and yelling at them may diminish their self-esteem and make them susceptible to bullying.

6. Work on gaining parental self-control. Parental self-control may seem difficult to achieve, but constant work on oneself will help you attain the level you need to maintain a healthy working relationship with you and your children.

7. Call out the trigger at the moment and talk yourself out of reacting. Always remember you are a work in progress.

REFLECTION QUESTIONS

From the "Seven Essential Factors list," pick the two you want to start working on this week. Write them down below.

_____

_____

_____

_____

_____

_____

_____

_____

_____

"A hot-tempered
person stirs up strife, but the slow
to anger calms a dispute" (Proverbs 15:18).

CHAPTER SUMMARY

- Managing and controlling your emotions when interacting with your child is key to purposefully parenting.

- Parenting triggers can be described as super reactive spots from within you that are activated by your child's words, behaviors, attitudes, or comments.

- Understanding your parenting triggers – our children remind us of ourselves and sometimes the very things we don't like about us. Therefore, when we see them exhibiting those behaviors, it becomes a trigger, and we flare up at the slightest display of it.

- Taking a deeper dive - Parenting puts a spotlight on you, and the audience is your family. They get to see you outside of the public view, and they see it all: your weak or strong moments.

- Be Self-aware - Because your children have the wrong attitudes, meltdowns, or throw tantrums does not mean you should join them. It is best to respond by being calm, not raising your voice. Be reasonable about whatever the issue might be.

»CHAPTER 8«

SMART EMOTIONS

No matter the situation, never let your emotions
overpower your intelligence - Kushandwizdom

To build and develop a healthy relationship with your children, you will need to embrace the power of self-control, taking charge of your emotions. This requires applying empathy and high emotional intelligence in your relationships. The focus of this chapter is for parents with teenagers. Your relationship with your children can either make them grow spiritually and emotionally mature or hinder them from growing at all. I say this because our children watch us and everything we do. I believe I discussed this extensively in the previous chapter when I said you are a mirror.

Understand this, my beloved brothers and sisters. Let everyone be quick to hear [be a careful, thoughtful listener], slow to speak [a speaker of carefully chosen words and], slow to anger [patient, reflective, forgiving]; (James 1:19)

A friend's son, Aiden, returned home from school where he was in first grade. He told both parents that he was bullied at school by a boy named Samson. He narrated the end-to-end story of what happened in school to his parents, how the boy slapped him, kicked him, and pulled down his pants.

The mom was so furious, she decided to email the teacher about the incident. She started the email by asking why the teacher didn't call them about what happened because they should know. She went on to narrate everything Aiden told them. She expressed her anger and frustration in writing and then blamed the teachers for not informing them. So one of the teachers responded and said that Aiden had the best day and there is no one by the name of Samson in his class.

The mom almost melted in embarrassment and shame. If you were in Aiden's parent's shoes, what would you do to Aiden? This is where emotional intelligence comes into play. Aiden's mom and dad put their heads together to figure out how to deal with this situation without breaking Aiden's spirit and to ensure he didn't do it again.

First, they prayed for the Holy Spirit to help guide them. The next thing they did was write a long email to apologize to the teacher. The theme you will notice from this story is that feelings matter a lot. Aiden's parents were really hurt by the lie, and they were embarrassed as well. I am sure this was an emotional rollercoaster neither of Aiden's parents had planned for.

Aiden's dad asked him why he lied, and he said he saw a cartoon series where somebody did that, so he copied it. He was disciplined by taking away his prized toy called Lego for some time.

What insights can be taken from this story?

1. Aiden's parents were mindful of their reactions and the emotions they were experiencing.
2. They both prayed.
3. They apologized to the teacher.
4. They tuned in to understand why their son lied.
5. They disciplined Aiden.

This is what emotional intelligence and empathy are about—being smart about how you are feeling. Notice the order of the steps Aiden's parents took; the last thing they did was discipline him. It was not the other way around. This way, they bought themselves some time to calm down, reflect, and respond instead of reacting.

Emotional Intelligence is about being smart about your emotions. John Gottman describes different types of emotions from a parent-child relationship; it starts with you. He said,

One needs to begin with oneself. It is important to understand one's own feelings about emotions and learn that self-understanding comes from recognizing one's own feelings. Emotions are our internal "GPS" through life. Opening up our own emotional world and being emotional is where we need to start, which confers huge gifts.

You need this in every season of your parenting, whether your child is a baby, toddler, kid, big kid, preteen, teenager, young adult, or adult. Emotional intelligence helps you control your thought process by carefully crafting your words before engaging in or starting a conversation with a defensive or moody child.

Empathy is the ability to put your feelings aside and see your child's point of view so you can connect and pass your message across in a way it can be heard. When you view situations and scenarios from your children's perspective, you are processing your emotions. "Nobody cares how much you know until they know how much you care."—Theodore Roosevelt

Meet April and Sam, parents of Eva (15-year-old child). April and Sam can't seem to understand why Eva is always moody and her attitude toward them. Eva thinks "there is no point in talking with her parents because they will never understand or see her perspective."

Let's pause.

Something is wrong here.

Would you agree?

April, Sam, and Eva's relationship is missing empathy toward one another and emotional intelligence. By applying high emotional intelligence is a critical element of forming healthy relationships. Your child may not repeat that same gesture to you, but you are the adult in the room; therefore, you must lead by example. As a parent, you can't automatically assume, "Here we go again with this behavioral issue or attitude." Every day, teens are faced with challenges and decisions that affect their emotional behavior.

The writer of Hebrews said:

> Discover creative ways to encourage others and to motivate them toward acts of compassion, doing beautiful works as expressions of love. This is not the time to pull away and neglect meeting together, as some have formed the habit of doing. In fact, we should come together even more frequently, eager to encourage and urge each other onward as we anticipate that day dawning. (Hebrews 10:24-25, Amplified)

The key to building a healthy relationship with your teenager is empathy and high emotional intelligence. Empathy and high emotional intelligence are two powerful ways to help you connect, reason, and care more about your child's feelings. No matter how tough children seem, their emotions are driving forces behind their behaviors. Therefore, it is vital to recognize this tool to help you decide based on rationality and not emotions when interacting with your child. It is a powerful way for parents and teens to bond on a personal level. These are moments when you can instill life values, principles, and lessons that will help build and encourage your child. The minute you try to put yourself into the world of your children, it signals you care about them.

Have Empathy and Emotional Intelligence in your daily toolbox. It is a powerful way to bond and connect on a deeper level. These are moments when you can instill life values, principles, and lessons that will help build and encourage your teenager. "Let no one seek only his good but that of the other person" (1 Corinthians 10:24). How can you apply empathy and emotional intelligence in your parenting approach? Listed below are six tips to help you get started:

1. Work towards applying empathy and emotional intelligence. This will help you recognize your children's emotions.
2. Think about your children's feelings.
3. Encourage them with stories and life lessons.
4. Build a better relationship through the power of communicating.
5. Learn more about your children.

"Finally, all of you be like-minded (united in spirit, sympathetic, brotherly, kindhearted, (courteous and compassionate toward each other as members of one household) and humble in spirit" (1 Peter 3:8).

APPLYING EMPATHY AND EMOTIONAL INTELLIGENCE

The principles and approach of emotional intelligence and empathy should be applied daily. Assuming April and Sam make a conscious effort to speak to Eva daily, Eva will automatically find it easy to confide and approach her parents. Below are three ways to show you care:

1. It will help if you are genuinely concerned about the emotional well-being of your child. Don't just do it when you want to find out or dig out dirt from your child or another person's child.
2. Tell them you are here for them. Use words of affirmation to draw them closer to you.
3. Ask your teenagers about ways you can help them overcome their emotional issues. Yes, it is a sensitive issue because teens are temperament-driven beings.

Being an adolescent can be stressful, psychologically demanding, and emotionally draining. What do I mean? It's a time when their brains undergo significant development while trying to grow. Because of this, your teenager will exhibit emotional, hormonal, and psychological behaviors.

It's hard to be in their shoes; therefore, as a parent, you need to be more empathetic and use high emotional intelligence when interacting with them. Your role at this time is significant because you will help them grow and understand their emotions can either make them or break them. Emotions are powerful and can be destructive when they direct us. You must help your child transition from adolescence to adulthood.

It is a powerful way to bond and connect on a deeper level. These are moments when you can instill life values, principles, and lessons that will help build and encourage your teenager. As I said before, the minute you try to put yourself into your child's world, it can be translated that you care.

Be Consistent

The principle and approach of emotional intelligence and empathy must be applied daily. If parents consciously speak to teenagers daily, they will automatically find it easy to confide and approach their parents. Below are four ways to show you care:

1. Be genuinely concerned about the emotional wellbeing of your child.
2. Use words of affirmation to draw your teenager closer to you.
3. Ask for feedback about how you are doing as a parent.
4. Learn to identify and understand your child's emotions.

John Gottman says,

> Most importantly, the child learns that one can be loved without being perfect. That feeling of unconditional love, of being able to repair negative interactions, of being mindful of your own emotions and those around you— that's a wonderful foundation upon.

With parental guidance, any child can build a fulfilling and successful life. You have to make a daily effort to show empathy to your child. Yes, you have struggles, responsibilities, and worries. You have matters that need addressing. Your plate is full. However, it is critical for parents to have empathy and emotional intelligence. They will help you have productive and coaching moments with your child. These life lessons will be experiences your teenagers will apply in the future and perhaps pass along to their children.

CHAPTER SUMMARY

- Having the ability to manage: Your relationship with your children can either make them grow spiritually and emotionally mature or hinder them from growing spiritually and emotionally.

- Emotional Intelligence is about being smart about your emotions.

- Empathy is the ability to put your feelings aside and see your children's point of view so you can connect and pass your message across to be heard.

- Empathy and high emotional intelligence are two powerful ways to help you connect, reason, and care more about your children's feelings.

- It's hard to be in their shoes; therefore, you need to be more empathetic and use high emotional intelligence when interacting with them as a parent.

≫ PART THREE ≪

MAKING IMPACTS

»CHAPTER 9«

LOVE ALWAYS

Parental love is the only love that is truly selfless,
unconditional, and forgiving - T.P Chia

When life feels too big to handle, hug your child. It's amazing how everything is put back into perspective when you are holding your whole world in your arms" (Proud Happy Mama). Love always, even when it is not convenient. Loving your children unconditionally is imitating god's love for you and then extending that same love to them every day and every moment. Do it when your children are in a good mood and when they are not in a good mood. Regardless of what mood your children are in, love them like Jesus Christ loves you and died for you.

You may say it is easier said than done. You are right. But with the help of the Holy Spirit, you can do it. Let us look at what God's love looks like and see the areas we can work on:

> Love is large and incredibly patient. Love is gentle and consistently kind to all. It refuses to be jealous when a blessing comes to someone else. Love does not brag about one's achievements nor inflate its own importance. Love does not traffic in shame and disrespect, nor selfishly seek its own honor. Love is not easily irritated or quick to take offense. Love joyfully celebrates honesty and finds no delight in what is wrong. Love is a safe place of shelter, for it never stops believing the best for others. Love never takes failure as defeat, for it never gives up. (1 Corinthians 13:4-7, The Passion Translation)

LOVE IS MEANS HAVING PLENTY OF PATIENCE.

What does it mean to be a patient parent? One day, you woke up late—I mean very late—and you have less than forty minutes to get all the kids up and ready for school. Your older son comes to you, "Mom, I can't find my shoes." Your daughter spills jelly on the fancy dress she was wearing to school for picture day. And you're expecting the bus to show up in fifteen minutes. You are extremely stressed out, frustrated, and yelling. You may be crying, upset, and just ready to crawl back into your bed. You wish you were dreaming.

Let's take a step back and look at this same scenario from a patient side. Being patient gives us an option to respond and not react. For example, can you let the bus driver go? Can you call into work late and drop off your kids on your way there with a high praise song in the background? Can you plan your day the night before? Every day will not go well. Some days will definitely be challenging. However, it is always important to assess the options you have available. This is the advantage of parents having and exercising patience. You can't always control circumstances and situations, but you can control how you react to them. Try patience.

Love is gentle and consistently kind to all. This is an area of strength for my husband. He is very soft-spoken as a whole, so when he speaks to the boys, softly. His voice level is the same, whether upset or when he is conversing with the boys. Over the years, I have watched how the boys respond to him and how they respond to me. I noted that my husband's approach worked better, so I tried to lower my volume from being super-up to lower. I decided to follow my husband's steps by maintaining the same level. Anytime I notice my volume going up, I count with my eyes closed or walk away. I am still working on this area of my communication.

Applying gentleness to our parenting is beneficial to our children and us, including reducing our blood pressure. Plus, when our kids grow up, and we tell them stories about the moments when they blew all the chances we gave them, lots of laughter will come out of that conversation.

Sarah Ockwell-Smith, the author of *The Gentle Parenting Book*, says,

> Gentle parenting isn't really about using specific methods. It's about an ethos and completely changing the way you think. It's more a way of being than a way of doing. Approaching any parenting situations with empathy for the child and trying to understand the reasoning behind their behavior, working together to change it positively and accepting what cannot be changed.

When you've called your children so many times or reminded them about cleaning their messy rooms with so many items on the floor, or your toddler gets you cranky because he doesn't do what he is told, your first instinct is to yell and tell them about themselves. At least, that's what I would do. You may not have the self-control to count or walk away. So how do you show patience in this instance? This is when you see the situation from the view of love by separating the behavior and your child.

Love does not traffic in shame and disrespect. No matter how little or old our children are, we must approach them with respect. They are human beings just like you and me. The difference is maturity and behavior. A friend was visiting her neighbor's house. The teenage son said something to the dad, which he translated as] disrespectful. The dad slapped this son in front of my friend. The teenage boy wasn't upset about the slap, but he was embarrassed about being hit while explaining something to his father.

Children naturally value parents. Their personalities may express that value in ways that seem to test limits, but understand every child seeks to learn how to navigate the world in the context of their parent's experiences. "Parents are the ultimate role models for children. Every word, every movement has an effect. No other person or outside force has a greater influence on a child than a parent."—Bob Keeshan.

There are many books out there that speak to parenting with love. My focus here is not to talk about how you discipline your children. However, when you discipline them, make sure it's coming from a place of love. You are not punishing the child. As you discipline your children, let it come from a place of love. Learn to separate your child as a person from the behavior you don't like. And when you've given them the consequences for their behavior, it is important to reset the situation with love. Laura Markham said, " Unconditional love isn't just what we feel. It's what the object of our love feels: love without strings attached. That means our child doesn't have to be or do anything in particular to earn our love. We love her exactly as she is."

> " Too often we forget that discipline really means to teach, not to punish. A disciple is a student, not a recipient of behavioral consequences
>
> — Daniel J. Siegel

A friend of mine, the day after she disciplines her children, she goes to their room early in the morning and prays for them. Then she kisses each of her children. She resets the situation with love. That is what you should endeavor to do when you are at a comfortable stage to speak about what happened. It is also important to know your own self and your style. Are you the type of person who can have a conversation immediately after an issue without hurting your child's feelings?

Are you a parent who needs time to calm down before you engage in a conversation with your child? This is a good question for you because you don't want to say something you will regret saying in the future. So you must know your approach. At a conference, a man shared a story about how his own dad would speak to him after he did something wrong. Instead of his dad addressing it immediately, his dad would wake him very early in the morning to talk about the issue from the previous day. The man said, his dad's approach was effective because every word would sink into his heart. It shows his dad has weighed all the

103

options and taking time to cool off before approaching him. This communication style was so effective that it made the man not repeat the same behavior next time because he didn't want the early morning lecture. Because of the man's experience, he applies the same approach to his children. Our children love us for who we are. Our children will copy the love we show them and display it on the outside.

CHAPTER SUMMARY

- Love always, even when it's not convenient
- Loving your children unconditionally is imitating God's love for you and then extending it to your children every day and every moment.
- Love is Patient
- You can't control circumstances and situations, but you can control how you react to them. Try patience.
- Love is gentle and consistently kind to all
- Love does not traffic in shame and disrespect
- No matter how little or old our children are, it's important that we approach them with respect. They are human beings just like you and me. The difference is maturity and behavior.
- Discipline with love
- Separate your child as a person from the behavior you don't like.

»CHAPTER 10«

KEY INGREDIENT

You'll never be a perfect parent.
But you can be a praying parent - Mark Batterson

Every dish requires salt as the key ingredient. Regardless of what type of food you make, this is the star ingredient in every food. All countries and continents rely on salt for food. If you don't apply salt to your cooking, it won't bring out the flavor, or your food will become tasteless. To effectively parent as Custodian appointed by God, you need key ingredients that will be your salt in every situation and every interaction with your children. This chapter will cover the key ingredients that all parents need to purposefully parent.

Maybe your understanding of parenting is based on your upbringing, your life experiences, and watching other people as they interact with their children. Your understanding can also be based on the training you have gone through in preparation for parenthood. Dr. Haseell, a pediatrician at the Pediatric Specialists Medical Group, captures the key ingredients from a child's point of view, he said: "If your child feels loved and has been reared in a stable and safe environment with a sense of consistency and structure, they will usually be well adjusted and happy." Like salt brings out the flavor in every food, prayer is the salt that makes your efforts grow. Now let's look at the key ingredients every Christian parent can apply.

PRAYER - THE STAR INGREDIENT

We need to lean on prayer as a way of communicating to God or speaking to Him about the lives we are custodians of. I cannot overstate the need to ask Him daily for help in your parenting approach. There is a saying the family that prays together stays together. I will take these same words and say parents who are connected with God in prayer will be less burdened by the responsibilities of parenting children.

I have learned over the years to wake up a few hours before the entire house is up. I do this to feed my spiritual self. Every day brings new opportunities and new challenges, so I must empty out yesterday, look to God for inspiration for the day in prayer, and study His Word. As humans, we are spiritual beings. Therefore, we need to seek God and ask for His input in all areas, including our careers, businesses, marriages, relationships, and parenting.

Imagine you spending more time in God's presence, how much knowledge, awareness, clarity, and spiritual understanding you will have. Picture reading your Bible, praying the scriptures aloud, and applying part of that prayer to yourself as a mother or father. When you pray for your children, spend more time praying for yourself to fulfill God's will in their lives. Ask the Holy Spirit to help you prepare your children for the future He has destined for them. You are only a vessel of honor God wants to use to kick off your children's destinies, so you need to stay plugged into God as your source of strength.

In high school, I ran track and field. There is a special race called the four-by-one relay. On the four-by-one team, there are four individual sprinters. There is the first leg, a second leg, a third leg, and the fourth leg. Using the four-by-one relay as a comparison, let us imagine God as the first leg. He gives you and your spouse the baton to run the next leg while He is still in the background, encouraging you to keep going. God places the baton in our hands so we can gently run the race of life with Him in the picture. Every day, we should see ourselves as that second leg to nurture and provide for our children - guiding their ways, showing them God's love, extending God's grace to them daily, teaching and guiding them in God's ways. We are to be good examples with morals and principles they can emulate, preparing the child for the third hand-off where they get to apply on their own what God has used us to do in their lives.

WHEN YOU NEED PRAYER

Being a mom can be challenging, overwhelming, fun-filled with laughter, meltdowns, and sometimes anxiety. These are moments you need God's supernatural help to lift you up in your spirit, to empower you, and give you the grace to go on. But one thing is required, you have to stay plugged in. For the fan to cool you down, you have to keep it plugged into the outlet.

At times we need to cool down. Things around us may look bad, our energy is low, and we are exhausted from the day-to-day tasks. These are moments when we need to stay plugged into the source of life: God. It's not easy, but we must cultivate the mindset of staying plugged into God as we pray and seek His input every day of our lives. If we are not connected, we may become overwhelmed. Our children are watching us to see how we will handle the stress in our lives.

> **"To be a Christian without prayer is like a lamp that's not plugged in.**
> — Daystar

Again, we don't know the future, but we know the One who owns their future. Listed below are the types of prayers you can pray as a parent by applying God's Word.

Pray for a Compassionate Heart

"You are always and dearly loved by God! So soak yourself

with virtues of God since you have been divinely chosen to be holy. Be merciful as you endeavor to understand others, and be compassionate, showing kindness toward all. Be gentle and humble, unoffendable in your patience with others". (Colossians 3:12, The Passion Translation)

Father, I thank You for loving me despite all my struggles and weaknesses. Thank you for your word that feeds my spirit. Thank you for choosing me as a parent for this precious gift You have put in my care. Father, help me to show kindness to my children. Help me be a gentle, humble, more compassionate parent, slow to be angry, in Jesus name (Amen).

Pray for a Mouth of Wisdom

"She opens her mouth in [skillful and godly] wisdom, And the teaching of kindness is on her tongue [giving counsel and instruction]" (Proverbs 31:26, Amplified).

Father, thank You for creating my mouth. I know there are moments when I have said the wrong words in anger and frustration to my children. Lord, please forgive me. Help me to have a mouth filled with wisdom. A mouth that will uplift my children and not pull them apart. Help me to be caring and gentler with my words when I speak to my children. Please give me counsel to speak with wisdom and not mislead my children in my ways. May I always lead them to You, in Jesus Name (Amen).

Pray for a Heart of Grace

"You do well and excel in every respect—in unstoppable faith, in powerful preaching, in revelation knowledge, in your passionate devotion, and in sharing the love, we have shown to you. So make sure that you also excel in grace-filled generosity" (2 Corinthians 8:7).

Dearest Father, thank You for unlimited access to the grace You have given me. Even though I don't deserve it, You provide me with grace daily. Thank You for Your unconditional love through grace. Lord, help me to extend this same grace daily to my children. To love them unconditionally as You love me. Lord, please transform my heart to be generous and full of grace. Help me to excel in this area of my parenting, in Jesus name (Amen).

Pray for a Home full of God's Love

"Remain in Me, and I [will remain] in you. Just as no branch can bear fruit by itself without remaining in the vine, neither can you [bear fruit, producing evidence of your faith] unless you remain in Me" (John 15:4).

Heavenly Father, thank You for Your gift of life in me and my home. Thank You for remaining in me every day, every hour, and every moment of my life. Lord, help me and my entire household to remain in You. Lord, I pray we will be connected to You as the true Vine of our lives. Help everyone in my house to serve You, connect with You, and be fruitful in You. Thank You for answering this prayer in Jesus name (Amen).

Staying plugged in requires our actions to be in line with our spiritual lives. Don't underestimate the power of prayer and placing it all at the feet of Jesus. Prayer can change our children and us. Parenting can be overwhelming, and prayer can help us release our burden to the One who gave us these gifts, but we have to stay plugged in.

We get better results when we place Jesus at the center of our lives, including our decisions and parenting. We are less stressed, as well as more joyful and peaceful in our hearts. Lean on and plug into prayers at all times. As you grow in your faith in God, so will your household grow as well. Can you envision your family growing in God's Word, ways, and wisdom? Can you visualize sharing each other's weaknesses and encouraging one another to keep growing? What a peaceful home that would be. And yes, it is achievable, but the tone and temperature depend on you and me.

CHAPTER SUMMARY

- Your understanding of parenting is based on your upbringing, lived experiences, and watching other people as they interact with their children.

- Lean on prayer as the key ingredient that brings out all the other flavors.

- Rely on prayer as a way of communicating to God or speaking to Him about this life we are custodians of. Ask Him to help you daily in your parenting approach.

- Plug into prayer because God places the baton in your hands, so you can gently run the race of life with Him in the picture.

- Have a heart of compassion and grace.

- Have a mouth of wisdom.

- Let your home be Jesus-centered.

»CHAPTER 11«

UNDERSTAND ALL SEASONS

Childhood Is a Short Season - Helen Hayes

A season (a time appointed) for everything and a time for every delight and event or purpose under the heaven. A time to be born and a time to die; A time to plant and a time to uproot what is planted" (Ecclesiastes 3:1-2). Would you agree that every mother and father will experience seasons as they proceed in their parenting journey? It will include rainy seasons, dry seasons, fall, winter, spring, and summer.

Can you picture your favorite and least favorite season of the year? Regardless of how your least favorite season is, you still have to go through it, and before you know it, it will be over. For me, my least favorite season is springtime when the allergies are out. Regardless of how I feel and how prepared I am with all my allergy medications, I still go through this season. Just like winter, fall, summer, and spring, our children will pass through various seasons on their way into adulthood.

The seasons are the focal point in this chapter and what you need to learn during each period. I will share the five seasons every parent will experience in the following pages - Serving season, sowing season, training season, mentoring/Autopilot Season, and the Tour Guide Season. You will find wisdom and practical advice as I explain some areas you should focus on.

Alison Gopnik, in her book, *The Gardener and the Carpenter*, captures a critical point for mothers and fathers to understand their role better. She says:

> **The carpenter parent** – "You should pay some attention to the kind of material you are working with, and it may have some influence on what you try to do. But essentially, your job is to shape that material into a final product that will fit this scheme you have in mind, to begin with".

> **The gardener parent** – "When we garden, on the other hand, we create a protected and nurturing space for plants to nourish it takes hard labor and the sweat of

our brows, with a lot of exhausted digging wallowing in manure."

I want you to pause and ask yourself these questions. Which of the two types of parents are you? Are you a gardener parent? A carpenter parent? Or are you indifferent about both seasons?

> **"Your Mind is a Garden,
> Your Thoughts are the Seeds.
> You can grow Flowers or weeds**
> – Osho

The gardener parent never stops working because a tree never stops growing. For a seed to grow into a tree, the gardener has to prepare the seed's environment. Once the seed has been planted, the gardener has to water and look after the seed to know if weeds are growing around it. This is the role of a father and mother.

Being a parent is about cultivating the soil (your heart) and feeding yourself with the right words (for me, it's God's Word). As you humble yourself in the presence of God, you gain more insight about yourself and areas of opportunities for you to improve upon; it's like a light shining through your heart. You have to grow in every stage and season of your parenting journey.

The parenting journey has five seasons: serving season,

sowing season, training season, mentoring/Autopilot Season, and the tour guide season. Regardless of what season you're in, you should always be a gardener who plants the right seeds. Allison Gopnik also says, "Parents are not designed to shape their children's lives. Instead, parents and other caregivers are designed to provide the next generation with a protected space in which they can produce new ways of thinking and acting."

Like anything else, every season a parent goes through requires prayer, faith, and hard work. Solomon, one of the wisest men in the bible, said, "for everything, there is a season, a time for every activity under heaven" (Ecclesiastes 3:1, NLT). I know there are many topics on the seasons of parenting, but I want to pivot it to help you understand your role. Every parenting season has a milestone before the next one comes around. Let's review each season and areas you can focus on.

Serving Season

Between the newborn stage to two years old, the child is the center of your world. The word "servant" tells it all. It is about serving. In this season of our parenting, our main focus is on serving the needs of our children constantly. Your key role during this season is connecting with your child, your spouse and maintaining self-care.

Sowing Season

Ages three to five years old is a critical season for your role as a parent and laying the right foundation. How is your relationship with Christ? Is it routine, or are you connected to Him? It's about you as the Sower.

It involves you sowing your time, patience and being incredibly involved with nurturing and providing for your child, emotionally, spiritually, and psychologically. You do the sowing of the seeds now, so later, the roots will grow. "Sow your seed in the morning and do not be idle with your hands in the evening, for you do not know whether morning or evening planting will succeed, whether this or that, or whether both alike will be good" (Ecclesiastes 11:6).

Here are five areas of focus:

1. Help shape your children's view of God. Study together to learn from their perspective. See where their understanding of God is and help them grow.
2. Know your parenting style and your spouse's parenting style as well. This will help you not to clash in the presence of your children. Parent on the same page as your spouse.
3. Good communication is key in this season.
4. Be willing to be flexible with the focus on being the adult. Remember, you are dealing with a kid, so you need grace.
5. Know your buttons and limitations. Be realistic and willing to grow in this journey.

Training Season

From ages six to eleven, you train your child and build

foundations that will help them become good citizens. Think about personal trainers. They don't only tell you what to do. They do it. In other words, they walk the walk and talk the talk. That way you can follow them.

You can't lead by speaking alone. Your actions matter as well. You will learn a lot about your strengths, weaknesses, and triggers during this season. Your words should be focused on clarifying, giving options, and applying the authoritative parenting style in full mode. What can you do at this stage?

Here are seven areas of focus:

1. Grow together in God's Word.
2. Pay attention to the needs of your children and their passion and gifts. What they like or dislike.
3. Spend more quality time with your kids in your busy schedule.
4. Be consistent with your love and do it unconditionally.
5. The key to discipline is to teach what is right from what is wrong. Before you discipline, ask yourself these three questions - Was this a mistake? Was this intentional? Was this a rebellious act?
6. Set limits, clear boundaries, and expectations. Don't assume your child knows what you expect or think.
7. Look for seminars or workshops that speak to you and your current stage of parenting.

Mentoring/Autopilot Season

You are the captain in this season from ages twelve to eighteen, but it includes a newbie co-pilot who wants to drive; however, they have zero flying hours (your child). You will experience turbulence, storms, and some fog. But not all flying conditions are red flags. You can't relax too much; you still have to keep your eyes ahead of you. Meaning, work on establishing a closer relationship with your child as you both are in the cockpit area.

How can you stay connected and engaged in the autopilot season? Consistently spend time with your co-pilots to coach them on navigating, so they gain more experience and hours before reaching the young adult years. Connecting is the key. You will have to invest more time in building a strong relationship. "Let us [unselfishly] love and seek the best for one another, for love is from God; and everyone who loves [others] is born of God and knows God [through personal experience]" (1 John 4:7, AMP). What is required of you?

Here are seven areas of focus:

1. Be prayerful in this season, and lean on prayer a lot. All the advice you give your teenager should include prayer.
2. You need wisdom in your daily interaction and seasoned conversations. You must have a balance between your emotions and your logic. It is called wisdom and empathy. You need to observe yourself more, become aware of your emotions, and work on regulating them more.

3. Asking more open-ended questions such as what have you learned from this experience? How do you plan to achieve this idea? What is the best solution to this issue? What is the most important thing to focus on here?

4. Watch your words because they can be internalized a lot in this season. Words are like eggs; once spoken, you cannot put them back together. It's okay to be angry; try and avoid speaking negatively into the life of your teenager.

5. Don't take anything personally. Be involved. You play a critical role in ensuring you fully understand and are staying engaged with your teenager. Teen years are stressful, demanding, and draining psychologically and emotionally.

6. Establish rules and expectations. For example, create a cell phone contract, curfews, grades, when your child can work, and chores around the house.

7. Help your children grow and nurture their gifts and talents.

Tour Guide Season

Ages 18 and up, you become the consultant by offering ideas, recommendations, counseling, and coaching. In this season, you get to relax and pray for yourself to be a vessel that will uplift and encourage your child. You get to sit back and become the listener, encourager, challenge their thoughts by positively influencing them, and asking your young adult child questions. When your child comes to you for advice or input and pulls from your wisdom, value it and create time to connect with them. You will have more of these sessions this season. This is where the fruits you planted in all the other seasons begin to grow.

Here are four areas of focus:

1. Your children will make mistakes, which can be costly. Your role is not to catch them but to help them understand what not to do and what to do the next time.
2. Be a prayer warrior and extremely sensitive to the Holy Spirit as He leads you to intercede for your children.
3. Never stop praying for your children. As a matter of fact, this is the season where your prayers go a long way in impacting your children. Your child will make decisions that will impact their lives, you may not be previewed of the decisions they make, but you can pray for God's will to always prevail in your children's life.
4. Respect their choices and stay away from parenting as you would in the training season.

The seasons of serving, sowing, training, mentoring / autopilot prepare you and your child for the tour guide season. That's why it's important to "Dedicate your children to God and point them in the way that they should go, and the values they've learned from you will be with them for life" (Proverbs 22:6, The Passion Translation). In Tracie Miles' devotional book *Enjoying the Seasons of Parenting*, she said,

> No matter which season we find ourselves in, let's treasure it and bask in the blessings it brings. Embracing

each season brings peace because we know we are right where God wants us to be and that He is preparing us for the season to come.

Therefore, we must take heed to this scripture: "Let us not become weary in doing good, for at the proper time we will reap a harvest if we do not give up" (Galatians 6:9, New International Version).

CHAPTER SUMMARY

- Our parenting journey will include rainy and dry seasons, fall, winter, spring, and summer.

- The gardener must first prepare the environment for that seed to grow before developing into a tree.

- Being a parent is about cultivating the soil (your heart). Feeding yourself with the right words (for me, it's God's Word).

- Serving Season: we are constantly serving the needs, wants, and desires of a newborn baby. Your key role during this season is connecting.

- Sowing Season: this is a critical season for your role as a parent and laying the right foundation. It is about you as the sower. It involves you sowing your time and patience, as well as being incredibly involved in nurturing and providing for your child emotionally, spiritually, and psychologically.

- Training Season: you are building foundations that will help your children become good citizens.

- Mentoring / Autopilot Season: You are the captain in this season, but it includes a newbie co-pilot who wants to drive but has zero flying hours.

- Tour Guide Season: You become the consultant by offering ideas, recommendations, counseling, and coaching. In this season, you get to relax and pray for yourself to be a vessel that will uplift and encourage your child.

»CHAPTER 12«

BUILDING
LASTING LEGACY

*Your greatest accomplishment may not be
something you do but someone you raise - Andy Stanley*

Your role is to apply faith and hope the seeds you've sown will grow on good ground. Legacy. "What is a legacy? It's planting seeds in a garden you never get to see" - Lin-Manuel Miranda. To leave a legacy for your children, their children's children, and then the generation after, you must answer these questions:

1. What values do I want to pass on to my children?
2. What do you envision?
3. What key principle do you want to make an impact on your children?
4. What are your goals and expectations of bringing up these children?

Legacy is what results from intentionally passing on sustainable behaviors and sound decision-making to the next generation. What do we need to do? What steps do we need to take? These thoughts and questions will help us understand the imprints we want to leave on the hearts of our children. To do this means you must be extremely sensitive to the Holy Spirit as He leads you. He will show you how to help your children actualize their unique gifts.

You are the vehicle to drive them to that point. It is a game-changer to look beyond what we do for our children and how we do it and purposely focusing on why we're doing it. A shift of our parenting perspective to one with a legacy in mind is critical. It's not easy, but this is the essence of being a parent and why you became a parent in the first place.

"The greatest legacy one can pass on to one's children and grandchildren is not money or other material things accumulated in one's life, but rather a legacy of character and faith."—Billy Graham

DEFINING YOUR FAMILY VALUES

What is important to you as a family, mom or dad? What experiences have you gained from your life until this moment that helps you grow? What costly mistakes have you made, learned lessons from, and want your children to avoid it at all cost?

I know a family that decided to do a value-based family project. The project was about creating values that everyone should follow and apply in their lives - in and out of the home. These values mirror what they want their children to also see in themselves. The mom posted six key family values around the house: in the kids' room, play area, and their family room. Here is a snapshot of the family values:

1. We will serve the Lord.
2. We will cherish God's Word in our lives and home.
3. We will tell each other the truth.
4. We will be kind to each other.
5. We will forgive each other.
6. We will listen to each other.

For my husband and me, the most valuable asset we can pass on to our children is our faith and belief in God as the Creator of all. Because our faith is the driving force that convicts, connects, and leads us, we must pass this baton to our children. This legacy of giving our faith to our children will also enable them to hand it to their children. We've identified the biggest thing we want to pass on to our boys through our journey so far: our faith and salvation in Jesus Christ and then our worldly goods.

Can you think of what is very important to you, and what is "one thing" you want to pass on to your children to help them in all areas of their lives? My husband and I introduced our children to our faith at a very early stage. As we go through the various seasons, we keep emphasizing the importance of our faith to them. I remember one time, actually, on several occasions, I asked my boys, why do you believe in Jesus? And sometimes I tell them, "Don't believe in God because we told you to; you must believe in God because you choose to." I echo that a lot so they can understand it clearly.

Stephanie Williams eloquently captures my thoughts this way "Every day you need to get a full dose of the Word and meditate on scripture, and if you discipline yourself and remain consistent, your faith will grow and mature and remember that God, the Word, and your faith, is a recipe for success." She nailed it, honestly.

Have a vision for your home

Because my husband and I are on the same page about our faith— this is what brought us together in the first place— creating a vision for our home was less of a burden, and we had few arguments about what those should be.

You may ask, what if my husband and I are not on the same page about our values? What do I do, and how do I come up with a vision for our home? I suggest you draft your recommendations of what you want the values in your home to be and propose them to your husband with an open mind for discussion.

What I'm trying to say is it's an easier and better approach. You open the door for discussion and to get your husband's contribution. This works out much better for all parties. Before you can have a vision for your children, you must have one for yourself. I went through this exercise five years ago. I asked myself questions about my mission and vision and how I would know if I made a difference with the gifts God has placed in me when I exit this world. I had to pray deeply. Afterward, I created a vision and mission statement for myself. My husband also has a vision and mission statement for himself.

The key point here is you must know why God created you. Once you are pursuing your purpose, you can carry your family along as well. How do you discover your purpose? I want to touch on this for a second. Ask yourself:

- What am I good at?
- What am I extremely passionate about?
- How can I use it to serve someone or a group of people around me?

It sounds very easy, but it requires a study of yourself. Moreover, I suggest you read other books on the market about finding your purpose and passion.

Finding our calling in life saves our children the struggle of finding their own. Because we have discovered how to find our own, we automatically hold their hands and lead them to learn and pursue theirs.

Think of how easy some things in their lives would be. Your child can be productive in every season of their lives, starting from childhood and moving into adulthood; that's legacy. This can be a vision for your home to help each other discover your gifts and talents as a family. It is a good recommendation for those who do not know what the vision of their family is. You can figure it out together.

My husband created one line of the vision for our home. I started the second line, so those two things are what we use to gauge ourselves and how we parent our children. This is a secret to purposefully raising giants and men and women with solutions for future generations, most importantly, vessels of honor for God in their generation.

Be a Student and Parent

Learn as much about yourself through your children's eyes. My kids are teaching me to be more patient. Becoming a parent is also a learning process for us in our parenting journey - raising mini-version of ourselves. Our two children teach us as we train them.

I am learning this more and more because our boys give us clues about how we should parent them. I keep learning this lesson - when you are not impatient or so consumed in your world and busy schedule, you are more effective in pointing your children in the right direction. It's not just talking; you need to do more listening as well.

FOUR WAYS TO BUILD A LEGACY FOR YOUR HOME

1. *Find the one thing that is important to you.* As I mentioned, in our home, our faith is very important to us. Therefore we parent with our faith in mind. We are not perfect, but we know we have room to grow. We understand this through faith.

2. *Value service.* Volunteering in your church or community. Find ways where you can serve with your children. You don't necessarily have to lecture them or introduce them to helping others. The more they see you serve, the more they learn that life isn't about them. They will consider what God wants to do through them. The lessons your children will learn from watching you serve will be forever imprinted in their hearts. They will learn to see beyond themselves and serve others.

3. *Prayer is a powerful tool all parents can teach their children.* However, you must first work on yourself and your prayer life before you can bring your kids on board. For example, a friend in her home has a small prayer room. When the kids can't find her on her bed very early in the morning because they woke up from a bad dream, they look for their mom in the prayer room. She tries to make a daily goal to spend time in God's Word. These actions that her children see drive them to grow in their faith as well. This mom isn't only talking the talk of prayer; she demonstrates it in her life,

and her children get to see it.

4. ***Knowing how busy your schedules are, we must carve out a time to focus on speaking and listening to each other during the week.*** Set aside time for a movie or game night or do an eat-out as a family day. This setting is a good way for our children to love and connect with us as we share and learn more about each other. A family friend has game night every Thursdays and movie night every Friday. This culture makes it very exciting for the children who look forward to those days. I've realized that you're in the same house with your spouse or your children does not mean you are connecting with each other. You may run into each other in the hallway. That's not a connection. The connection I am speaking of is when you grow together.

CHAPTER SUMMARY

- Defining your family values
- Look around you and see what helps you to be better versions of yourself daily. This is the most valuable asset you can pass on to your children.
- Have a vision for your home
- The key point here is to discover why God created you, and once you are pursuing it, you can carry your family along as well.
- Be a student parent
- Learn as much about yourself through the eyes of your children.
- Prayer is a powerful tool you can teach your children to use, but first, you must work on yourself and your prayer life before you can bring your kids on board. Or you all do grow together as a family

»» CONCLUSION ««

GOD CHOSE YOU

To be in your children's memories tomorrow,
you have to be in their lives today - Barbara Johnson

Becoming good parents start with first understanding what our roles are and the learning opportunities along the way. Then we will have a full understanding of our calling as custodians. The moment we shift our understanding from just parenting to doing it purposefully as raising our children for God's purpose. It brings meaning to our role.

Becoming a good parent starts with first understanding your roles and the learning opportunities along the way.

Throughout this book, we have explored different ways to be purposeful parents, different dimensions of our roles as parents, and becoming custodians of God's gifts. Having a helicopter view of ourselves as parents is key to purposeful parenting. When we see the bigger picture by looking beyond our children's imperfections and focusing on ourselves, what we say, how we say it, and what we do, we will grow and become conscientious parents.

Parenthood is a calling, and parenting is the work we do toward that calling. It is all about directing the paths of our children and pointing them in the right direction. We must know where we want them to go.

In part one, we learned that you must fulfill a purpose in your child's life, and only you can fulfill it as a custodian, not anyone else. As parents, we are called into lifelong ministry to express and demonstrate God's love in our lives by extending it to our children and in our homes. The call to parent is about understanding you are preparing your children for God to use them as vessels of honor for their generation every day.

They will solve humanitarian problems, become inventors, entrepreneurs, leaders, artists, professionals, and provide whatever solutions God has placed in their hands. We are to lay the right foundation in every season, at every stage of the child's life, and in our lives as well. God has given you the blueprint to build this foundation, His Word for you to learn from. Apply wisdom-based parenting. You are not perfect, and your children are not perfect. There will be situations that move you to your core or things your children do that will rock your emotions. The key to unlocking this is to learn not to react to that situation. You must be dependent on God to help you in your parenting journey.

We are called to serve and hand-picked by God to nurture and provide for the gift before us. That call is to raise our children as disciples for Christ. You are called to serve as an ambassador of God to your child and in your home. It will take time and energy. You are not alone. God is always on your side. It is a big responsibility, and it takes your heart to do it well, but God has equipped you for the journey.

In part two, we explored the foundation. Foundations are critical to the security of a building. If it is well defined and strongly built, you can be sure the building will stand when challenges come. What's your foundation with Christ-like? Is it strong or shaky? Is it on solid rock or sinking sand? If you establish your foundation on Christ, your children will be established in Him as well. Listed below are six pillars that will help us in our journey as parents:

1. Pillar 1 – Pray for yourself and your child
2. Pillar 2 – Teach them God's Word
3. Pillar 3 – Apply Wisdom
4. Pillar 4 – Be Intentional
5. Pillar 5 – Be Accessible
6. Pillar 6 – Be a Positive Role Model

We are mirrors that our children see themselves through. They are like sponges; they soak up what they see in you. You must not forget this. Everything you do is viewed and internalized by your child. Our parenting styles play a significant role in our children's lives and how they walk in the truth. When we manage our triggers: our feelings, things that get us upset, and so forth, we become better mirrors.

It is important to be smart with our emotions by looking at situations through different lenses and away from our feelings. To achieve this, we must have high emotional intelligence and empathy. It is key to building healthy relationships and having a peaceful home.

In part three, we focused on having a lasting impact. It starts with love, even when it is not convenient, and the fruits of passion. We have to be intentional. We must always pray for ourselves, how we parent, and God to lead us to make decisions that will positively influence our children. Stay connected to the source—God Himself.

We will experience four seasons in the parenting journey: serving season, tour guide and the tourist season, mentor and coach season, and friendship season. Regardless of what season you're in, you should always be a gardener who plants the right seeds. Lastly, it is all about making disciples for Christ. That requires us to become footprints for our children to follow to pursue their own purposes in life.

The time between giving birth to your child and growing

up into young adults is very short. As they pass through our homes and lives, it is important to see ourselves as vessels of honor. It is a privilege to be a parent, to become part of history by preparing these children for their own destinies. Let's not get too bogged down with controlling and trying to mold or shape them in a certain way. Our focus is raising them in God's way so they can raise their own children in God's way. It has a ripple effect from generation to generation.

When you see your children now, what do you desire for them? What actions are you taking toward that desire? This book was designed to help you look at parenting through the lens of God giving you a gift – your child to look after as part of your earthly duties. It is a temporary yet critical assignment of raising a human being. What are you willing to change about yourself? What would you do better? Remember, your parenting goal should be raising disciples for Christ, and you don't have to be a perfect Christian to achieve this.

I close with the following scriptures,

"He has told you, O man, what is good; And what does the Lord require of you. Except to be just, and to love [and to diligently practice] kindness (compassion), And to walk humbly with your God [setting aside any overblown sense of importance or self-righteousness]?" (Micah 6:8)

"And the Spirit of the Lord shall rest upon him, the Spirit of wisdom and understanding, the Spirit of counsel and might, the Spirit of knowledge and the fear of the Lord" (Isaiah 11:2).

"Ask, and it will be given to you; seek, and you will find; knock, and it will be opened to you. For everyone who asks receives, and the one who seeks finds, and to the one who knocks it will be opened" (Matthew 7:7-8).

"Understand this, my beloved brothers and sisters. Let everyone be quick to hear [be a careful, thoughtful listener], slow to speak [a speaker of carefully chosen words and], slow to anger [patient, reflective, forgiving]" (James 1:19).

APPENDIX

ACKNOWLEDGMENTS

To my creator, who has called me to inspire and empower parents with the gifts and talents He has given. I am so thankful to be a vessel to deliver this life-transforming message to myself and all the parents He has called to be custodians of His gifts.

Adeola, my amazing husband and best friend of 14 years, my closest confidant, encourager, and mentor, challenges me to push forward. You are a man after God's heart and an amazing custodian of the two gifts God gave us. May you continue to grow in your wisdom and understanding with God and man. In Jesus name. You have taught me the value of family time and better ways to raise our amazing boys to be who God has called them to be, solutions for their generation, and to pursue their passion.

To my sons, Fiayosi Isaac and Ayowade Gideon Adefemi, thank you for helping me grow in my faith and always challenging me daily with your questions and sometimes your unspoken words in moments of my strengths and weaknesses. This book was written from all the lessons you have taught me and still teach me about growing to become the tool that directs you in the path God has created you for.

To my mentor, P.G, thank you for always being an inspiration to maintain momentum, to be relevant and significant with the gifts God has given me. You are always there for me, responding to my requests and making time for me in your busy schedule. It's one thing to have a passion, but it takes a committed mentor to help birth the vision. Thank you for all you do for me.

To my amazing family and confidant, a big thank you for your support, encouragement, and for believing in me always. I could not do this without your critique and valuable insights.

To all parents in the world. Thank you for purchasing this book to grow in your journey as custodians of God's gifts. The call to parenting is a big task, and it can be overwhelming and exciting. The key to being purposeful starts with you connecting with the One who has called you to parent. May you fulfill your calling and make disciples for God's kingdom.

»ABOUT THE AUTHOR «

Toyin Adefemi is an author, speaker, parent, coach, teen specialist, emotional intelligence coach, NLP (Neuro-Linguistic Programming) Practitioner, and lover of God.

Toyin is married to her Ademi (my crown), her best friend of 14 years. She's a proud mom of two amazing boys. She is driven with a passion for impacting parents with insights into God's

Word and inspirations by empowering every parent one home at a time.

She helps all parents see the bigger picture, view parenting as a calling, and provide a healthy foundation to launch each child's vision and purpose. She empowers parents to:

- Raise emotionally intelligent, approachable, spiritual, and resilient children
- Lay a healthy foundation to launch your children's gifts and talents
- Build the critical pillars of leading, nurturing, providing, and discovering their children's needs
- Be purposeful in their parenting journeys

As a speaker and parent coach, she is dedicated to helping parents build better relationships, communicate and share lifetime memories with their children. She also empowers parents to embrace their parenting journey with grace.

Her belief is that our sons must flourish in their youth like well-nurtured plants. And our daughters must be like graceful pillars carved to beautify a palace.

How She Serves:

Regardless of your group's size: big or small, Toyin would be honored to come and speak at your upcoming event or program. Her inspirational speaking extends to schools, faith-based organizations, teen conferences, parent groups, and community organizations.

»NOTES«

This section captures all the additional tools and resources used in this book. It is almost impossible to review all the links and books referenced here to gain additional tools. Because mistakes may occur while citing each resource, if you do see any wrong citation, please feel free to email toyin@thepsprojects.com so these errors can be fixed immediately.

Introduction

1. Merriam-Webster. (n.d.). Parenthood. In *Merriam-Webster.com dictionary*. Retrieved March 12, 2021, from https://www.merriam-webster.com/dictionary/parenthood
2. Merriam-Webster. (n.d.). Parenting. In *Merriam-Webster.com dictionary*. Retrieved March 12, 2021, from https://www.merriam-webster.com/dictionary/parenting

3. New Living Translation 2015. Biblegetway. Retrieved March 19, 2021, from https://www.biblegateway.com/passage/?search=Psalm%2032%3A7-9&version=NLT

Chapter One

1. Elizardi, E. (2012, March 05). Parenting Is Calling! How Will You Answer? Psychology Today. https://www.psychologytoday.com/us/blog/parent-pulse/201203/parenting-is-calling-how-will-you-answer

2. Rainey. D. (2015, January 21). Parenting as a Calling. Family Life. https://www.familylife.com/podcast/familylife-today/parenting-as-a-calling/

3. Miles. T. (2014, May 23). Enjoying the Seasons of Parenting. Proverbs 31 Ministries. https://proverbs31.org/read/devotions/full-post/2014/05/23/enjoying-the-seasons-of-parenting

Chapter Two

1. Gerten, K. (2020, April 23). You've Got This! Parenting Quotes to Inspire. Youth Dynamics. https://www.youthdynamics.org/youve-got-this-parenting-quotes-to-inspire/

2. Breedlove, A. (Date Unknown). Planting Seeds Bible Study for Kids. In All You Do. https://inallyoudo.net/planting-seeds-bible-study-for-kids/

Chapter Six

1. Sánchez, J (2009, November 11). The Goal of Biblical Parenting. Christain Living. https://www.thegospelcoalition.org/article/the-goal-of-biblical-parenting/

Chapter Nine

1. Markham, L (2014, March 02). 5 Secrets to Love Your Child Unconditionally. Psychology Today. https://www.psychologytoday.com/us/blog/peaceful-parents-happy-kids/201403/5-secrets-love-your-child-unconditionally
2. Ockwell-Smith, S. (2021) *The Gentle Parenting Book: How to raise calmer, happier children from birth to seven* Little Brown Book Group Limited.

Chapter Eleven

1. Miles, T (2014, May 23). Enjoying the Seasons of Parenting. Proverbs 31 Ministries. https://proverbs31.org/read/devotions/full-post/2014/05/23/enjoying-the-seasons-of-parenting
2. Bristow Sidney (n.d). Unknown. Retrieved May 6,2021 from https://i.pinimg.com/originals/ea/27/ab/ea27ab7e1d44db422bd961a152b75d42.jpg
3. Hassell, D (2016, May 06). The Key Ingredients to Effective Parenting. http://www.psmgfl.com/blog/post/the-key-ingredients-to-effective-parenting.html

Made in the USA
Middletown, DE
16 May 2022